Special Needs Provision

Assessment, Concern and Action

Geof Sewell

CASSELL

Cassell

Wellington House
125 Strand
London WC2R 0BB

127 West 24th Street
New York
NY 10011

First published 1996

British Library Cataloguing-in-Publication Data
A catalogue record for this book is available from the British Library.

ISBN 0–304–33802–8 (hardback)
    0–304–33803–6 (paperback)

Printed and bound in Great Britain by
Biddles Ltd, Guildford and King's Lynn

Contents

Acknowledgements

My thanks go to the many special teachers I met on my LEA research project, to Pauline Maddison, Alistair Robertson and Linda King, to Margaret Bond and the teachers who attended her courses on the Code, and to the staff of the survey schools, especially Joyce Bailey and Pat Casey. I would like to thank Len Barton of Sheffield University, Tony Booth of the Open University and Michael Farrell of the South Bank University who read earlier drafts of the text and helped me with their ideas and comments. Any faults or failings remain my responsibility. I have endeavoured to protect the anonymity of the pupils, through changing and amalgamating identities – though I would like to name Avril, Duane and Caroline as having done most to share with me the realities of special education. Without the patience and love of Lois and Rachel, there would have been no time to reflect and no Monday nights to piece the book together.

Editorial foreword

This is a book for practitioners written by a teacher with long experience of special needs provisions in mainstream schools. It is particularly addressed to the SEN Coordinators who are now struggling, sometimes against heavy odds, to fulfil their statutory responsibilities and to enhance good practice in all primary and secondary schools in the country.

This is no mere cookbook or beginner's guide to the *Code of Practice on the Identification and Assessment of Special Educational Needs*. Although he adopts a very positive stance towards the Code, Geof Sewell deploys his detailed knowledge of ordinary schools to provide detailed information on good practice, illuminated by many examples of schools and individual pupils, drawn from a wider survey. Much of this good practice was developed by schools themselves long before the Code, often with little external support, and sometimes in the face or apathy or resistance from their own staff. The book provides encouraging examples of how obstacles have been overcome.

The Code of Practice has been warmly welcomed but one message of the book is that schools must go beyond the Code if they wish to develop truly inclusive education. In some respects, the Code perpetuates a defect model of special needs by concentrating on the difficulties experienced by different categories of pupils and by emphasizing differences between pupils with and without special needs. On the other hand, it provides valuable guidance on how schools as organizations can restructure their management and encourage cooperation and partnership among all members of staff to achieve a more accessible curriculum for all pupils and not just those with special needs. Special needs has to be demystified and seen as everyone's responsibility rather than that of a new generation of specialists.

Although, as Geof Sewell notes, the publication of the Code was not matched by the provision of training opportunities, its implications for staff development have now been spelled out in the Special Educational Needs Training Consortium report *Professional Develop-*

ment to Meet Special Educational Needs (1996). This report lists the knowledge, skills and understanding needed by all teachers in every sector of education, ranging from the newly qualified teacher through induction to all continuing professional development. It includes the competencies required by SENCos, as well as those needed by teachers working with pupils with specific identified needs in any sector of provision.

It is clear that the initiative for staff development now lies firmly with schools themselves, in partnership with LEAs and higher education. Geof Sewell's book will provide an invaluable resource to schools in examining and extending their practice.

Professor Peter Mittler
University of Manchester
June 1996

Introduction

THE READERSHIP

This book is primarily designed for Special Needs Coordinators and mainstream teachers to use together, as a basis for discussions about the assessment, inservice work and strategic planning for special provision. It follows the sweeping and predominantly positive changes that have come about since the publication of the *Code of Practice on the Identification and Assessment of Special Educational Needs* (DfE, 1994a). The Code is probably the most significant official publication in the field of mainstream special education since the Warnock Report (DES, 1978). It elaborates on and refines many of the Warnock Committee's proposals, but it also reconciles them with subsequent educational reforms. For some schools, including many of those described in the book, the implementation of the Code has meant very minor changes. For others, though, it can appear daunting. This book sets out to offer a stimulating but not uncritical guide to emerging good practice in the SEN field that:

- reflects the daily pressures of teachers' working lives;
- answers their concerns about disadvantaged, disabled and difficult pupils;
- shows them how to prevent learning difficulties;
- helps them to work more effectively with colleagues, other professionals, parents, pupils and school governors;
- encourages them to look beyond the existing Code to their concerns for their more vulnerable pupils.

RECONSTRUCTING THE CODE

Before the present Code of Practice was published, an initial draft was circulated for a brief period of consultation. Many commentators felt that the first draft represented a watershed, but that it should be slimmed down and revised. This duly happened. There was insufficient time to trial the proposals, however, and when the final draft was published it was greeted with similar ambivalence. Some, like Philippa Russell (1994), with a special concern for parents, thought of it as breakthrough. For some teachers, like Jane Harvey (1995), it appeared to build on 'existing procedures'. Others, like Dalton (1994) and Bibby (1994), articulated the anxieties of many staff. The more sceptical teachers were raising questions such as:

- Would schools spend so much time identifying and assessing special needs that they would have less to spend on prevention or provision?
- Would the Code lead to greater labelling and stereotyping, reducing expectations rather than raising them?
- Would the structure of the Code enable schools to rid themselves of low attaining or troublesome pupils, thereby slowing the progress of integration?
- How could hard-pressed teachers be motivated to make even greater efforts on behalf of the most disadvantaged, without extra resources?

This book will argue that, helpful though the present Code is, it should only be seen as a second draft. There are still ways in which the procedures of identification and assessment adopted by many schools and LEAs in response to the Code could be simplified and the paperwork reduced – while still satisfying the demands of OFSTED inspectors. These have become clearer in the months that followed publication and they are outlined in Chapter 2.

The main aim of the book, though, is to encourage a more creative and questioning approach to the *structure* of the Code. The Code focuses primarily on the identification and assessment of pupils with special needs. As many special educators have found over the years, these cannot be regarded as separate skills, but must be seen as part of the cycle of prevention and provision. This has led some to argue that there should not be five stages in the assessment procedures as the Code suggests, but six. Some schools are referring to a hypothetical *Stage Zero* or Stage Nought, which would include such preventive issues as:

- a good liaison with cluster schools;
- a review of whole-school assessment policies, to re-evaluate the place of SEN identification;
- a review of staff meetings to ensure regular consultation about pupils with learning difficulties;
- the involvement of the whole staff in the development of oracy skills;
- the training of the whole staff in reading recovery, etc.

These schools would argue that the Code is too narrowly focused. It does not reflect sufficiently the concerns of actual teachers. There are many teachers in today's mainstream schools, whose views are reported in this book, who share an unease about the apparent growth in social divisiveness and the ways this can be reflected in schools. They want to see more children from special schools integrated in the mainstream. Given the opportunity, these members of staff will often indicate a willingness to teach small groups of statemented pupils or work with them in well-supported classes – and gain considerable professional satisfaction from doing so. They are also concerned about the problems that increasing numbers of low attaining pupils appear to be having with basic skills. They want to be shown how to help pupils to meet basic standards in reading, spelling and maths. They are anxious about the effects that changing employment, income and family patterns seem to be having on the behaviour of their pupils and the strain this is placing on their own classroom management skills. They want to learn and they want more inservice training on SEN issues.

The main theme of the book is that many of these concerns can be harnessed, through coordinated inservice and staffing strategies. Teachers who are given the chance to learn how to deliver special provision – through teaching basic literacy or supporting statemented pupils in mainstream, for instance – can learn how to assess special needs in the process. This can enable them to take a more positive attitude towards these children's learning and so prevent difficulties arising for other pupils through informed classroom interventions. Such staff might take a different view of the structure of the Code. Some of the most distinctive phrases in the Code describe the borderlines between the various stages in the assessment procedures – such as *thresholds* and *triggers*. These teachers might be less likely to see these borderlines as the door to further and ever more sophisticated assessments, or as triggers, which could shoot pupils out of mainstream provision.

This book is largely based on work the author has been carrying out in developing the concept of special needs coordination since the original definitions in the early 1980s. Most of the material derives from the author's own school; but the book also includes additional data from a research project carried out among eight primary and secondary schools as part of a northern LEA's moderation exercise on definitions of the stages of assessment. The schools were chosen as centres of excellence in mainstream special provision, but they were also seen as representing the full range of educational and social deprivation. Some were situated in inner city areas whose unemployment rates were over 80 per cent; others were urban or suburban schools in areas which were much closer to national norms. One was included in the OFSTED list of excellent schools; another was quoted by the Basic Skills Agency as an example of good practice in the year of the survey.

With LEA support, it was possible to carry out interviews with headteachers, Special Needs Coordinators, classroom teachers, psychologists and LEA officers. These were followed up in an LEA training course, involving half the LEA's SENCos and a wide range of interested mainstream staff. The seminars and discussions helped to refine and elaborate some of the original ideas. Through the moderation survey, it was also possible to make contacts with LEA officers and psychologists in other parts of the country. These tended to suggest that the ideas, doubts and questions raised by the implementation of the Code in one small area were shared by teachers from across the country.

What emerged was a sense of shared priorities. The major issue for current teachers concerned with mainstream special provision was *basic literacy*. Not a single interviewee regarded any other issue as having greater priority in mainstream special provision. This finding seems to have been borne out in national surveys carried out by the Basic Skills Agency (Pateman, 1995). The second most important issue to emerge in our study was *behaviour*. There were a very few exceptions to this: one or two staff saw the other basic skills – especially maths – as more important than behaviour. The third set of priorities included *maths, spelling and oracy*; the fourth was the *integration* of statemented pupils, and the fifth was the *support* of other non-statemented pupils, such as those with speech, language, hearing, visual or health difficulties. Some schools also expressed the view – controversially but with great conviction – that *more able* and gifted pupils should be included in both staged assessment and special provision. Others, particularly from urban and inner city secondary schools, also regarded *attendance* as a special needs issue.

In other words, many schools had maintained and developed their sense of concern about special needs, despite shifts in government education policies and changes in the social and economic climate, since the concept of special needs received its official definition in the Warnock Report (DES, 1978). They had been quietly working away on their own preventive measures. These did not appear to feature in the second draft of the Code, so a new stage, Stage Zero, had to be created. Despite pressures to cut back on timetabled special provision, these schools had involved a wide range of staff in withdrawal work with small groups or in-class support. This had enabled these teachers to identify children with special needs in their own classes and provide them with more appropriate materials and classroom activities. Such staff could be relied on to make their own initial assessments of special needs – which could then be easily adapted to provide what the Code saw as its first stage. Having identified the children who were failing to thrive within the ordinary classroom, these schools had a clearly developed policy of involving additional support – from non-teaching assistants, parent helpers, special needs assistants (SSAs), mainstream staff, trained SEN specialists from within the school and LEA support services, psychologists and other outside agencies – which the writers of the Code saw as belonging to their second and third stages. Many of these schools had had some experience of working together with staff from other schools to-wards a new consensus on descriptors of special needs, prescriptions of special provision and the borderlines between them.

THE STRUCTURE OF THE BOOK

All staff interviewed emphasized their support for further SEN training – both for SEN Coordinators and for the full range of mainstream teachers. They appreciated the guidance they were receiving from existing books and courses on the Code. But what they really wanted was a chance to clarify their own roles and responsibilities, to discuss the emerging issues as they affected their own schools and to reflect on existing good practice. Subsequent discussions with teacher trainers, newly qualified staff and students have indicated that entrants to the profession would also appreciate a clear, accessible and critical commentary on the development of coordinated special provision in the aftermath of the Code.

The format of each chapter is broadly similar:

- Introduction;
- Objectives of each chapter;
- A series of discussions on the main issues;
- Reflections on existing good practice in the survey schools;
- Teacher or management tasks for inservice work;
- Feedback on practical teaching and management issues;
- Pupil perspectives;
- Summary.

The book starts by reviewing the role of the Special Needs Coordinator – a major theme in the Code – from its inception to the current position in contemporary research and in the survey schools. Chapter 2 looks at staged assessment, as envisaged in the Code, ways in which the paperwork can be simplified and the strategies that LEAs are adopting to achieve greater consistency about stage boundaries through the process of moderation.

The chapters following raise the kinds of concern that the teachers in the survey believed to be particularly pressing:

- the problem that some pupils with special needs have with speaking and listening;
- the perceived decline in reading skills among the less able, and ways to overcome it;
- the inservice training needed to help colleagues develop more effectively differentiated materials, activities and groupings;
- the particular needs of talented and more able pupils;
- emotional and behavioural difficulties;
- attendance;
- the integration of statemented pupils.

These chapters also offer a staffing and inservice training strategy which is grounded on some of the original definitions of coordinated special provision, that can harness the concerns of mainstream teachers, and that seems to accord with the work of other researchers/practitioners.

The book concludes with an analysis of the kinds of beliefs and working practices that enable schools to maintain and develop their work with children who have special needs. It is clear, for instance, that mainstream teachers working with disadvantaged children have been witness to radical changes in the years that have followed the definition of that term by Warnock. The gap between rich and poor has widened and the children of the poorest families have been hit by rising unemployment, low wages and insecure employment. At the level of the individual child, there is very little connection between learning difficulties and poverty, of course; some of the most affluent pupils have reading difficulties or disabilities, while some of the poorest go to university. However, there is a strong relationship between the proportion of poorer children in a school and the incidence of learning difficulties. Those with greater numbers of children in receipt of free school meals tend to have the highest numbers of poor readers. At the same time as the differences between rich and poor have grown, changes in family structures have accelerated. These have played their part in generating emotional and behavioural difficulties at all levels in society. Many staff in the survey schools were concerned about a combination of familial and economic trends, about the ways they had contributed to psycho-social changes in children and about their effects on the learning and behaviour of children with special needs.

Many governmental reforms in education have also affected the context within which special provision operates. Increasing competition between schools has meant greater polarization. 'Inclusive' schools with favourable reputations for their work with children with learning and behavioural difficulties are gaining more of them. A reputation for an increasing number of these pupils can have the effect of deterring the parents of the more able. Despite these pressures, some of the survey schools have clearly been able to show 'added value' among their mainstream pupils, including their highest and lowest attainers – and their integrated pupils with statements of special needs. These 'inclusive schools' had a set of beliefs that not only sustained special provision through some turbulent years, but may continue to help them survive the effects of market forces on the most vulnerable children in society.

Special Needs Coordinators

INTRODUCTION

The *Code of Practice on the Identification and Assessment of Special Educational Needs* (DfE, 1994a) adds a vital figure to the essential complement of schools – the SENCo, or Special Needs Coordinator. Every mainstream school is now to include a 'designated teacher' who will be responsible for:

- the day-to-day operation of the special needs policy;
- overseeing the identification and assessment of special needs;
- coordinating special provision;
- advising and contributing to the INSET of staff;
- liaising with parents and outside agencies.

The role of Special Needs Coordinator arose in the aftermath of the Warnock Report (Sewell, 1982; Bines, 1986). The Committee made no mention of it and Mary Warnock herself would suggest that there is little 'need' for SENCos in many schools (Warnock, 1994). This chapter argues that the same forces which led to the earliest definitions – the underfunding of teacher retraining, the marginalization of mainstream slow learners and the lack of government commitment to the integration of pupils from special schools – still pertain. These have affected the way that the Code of Practice has been reinterpreted in the schools that were chosen for the local research project on the moderation of definitions of the Code's Stages of Assessment (Robertson *et al.*, 1995) and in schools and LEAs contacted subsequently as part of the national research project. Chapter 1 discusses these structural forces – as well as Mary Warnock's critique – from historical, international and legal perspectives and asks:

- What are Special Needs Coordinators?
- How did the role arise and develop?
- How does their role differ from that of other middle managers in schools?

- How can they enable mainstream colleagues to meet the challenges of the Code of Practice and of the next few years?

OBJECTIVES

By the end of this chapter, you will have reviewed:

- recent changes in SEN provision in your school
- the role of the SEN Coordinator in your school
- your school's SEN policy statements.

DISCUSSION: HISTORICAL PERSPECTIVES

The notion of the Special Needs Coordinator embodies a practical, British response to an international concern about the pace of integration and the cycle of labelling and low expectations affecting mainstream low attainers. Although many of the functions of the Coordinator are outlined in the Warnock Report, the Committee did not see that there was any need to enumerate them or allocate responsibilities to any single teacher. Liaison with parents and outside agencies was for the 'named person'; liaison with staff for the headteacher, an advisory teacher or an 'experienced teacher'. I was one of the first to realize the importance of bringing all these roles together, to attempt a definition and to outline a philosophical justification (Sewell, 1982).

It has been argued that the Warnock Committee had been allowed to 'side-step' the issues of labelling, low expectations and integration from its inception. The Committee was set up in 1974, at a time when, according to Professor Ron Gulliford – the man who first defined the term 'special educational needs' – 'every right thinking teacher believed in integration'. It may therefore seem surprising that the brief given to the Committee by the then education secretary Margaret Thatcher did not include the words 'labelling' or 'low expectations' or 'integration'. The Committee was to review 'educational provision ... for children handicapped by disabilities of body or mind, taking account of the medical aspects of their needs, together with arrangements to prepare them for entry into employment ... [and] consider the most effective use of resources'.

At the time, it was clear to many researcher/practitioners such as myself that if the long-term goals of integration and a more effective education for pupils with learning difficulties were to be met, mainstream special education would need to be 'reshaped'. Every member of the profession would need to redefine their roles and their teaching commitments and adopt new methods of assessment and differentiation. This would have required a massive and costly retraining programme. However, in the discussions that followed Warnock, the government reiterated its 'continuing financial constraints'. The Report was not going to be shelved – neither was it going to be followed up with any large-scale retraining initiatives, unlike in other countries or regions at the time.

REFLECTIONS

- How many staff in your school feel inadequately prepared to identify and assess special needs?
- How many staff in your school have undertaken an accredited SEN training course?

FEEDBACK

In Italy, by contrast, the government decided (L 4 Agosto 1977 n. 517) that all special schools were to close, which they did on 1 January 1978. Pupils with recognized disabilities and learning difficulties were immediately placed in mainstream schools with certificates which entitled them to a given number of lessons per week of individual support from specially trained support teachers. A huge and expensive training programme was initiated for these *sostegni*. They were given a further one or two years' training to provide differentiated support materials for individual pupils with learning difficulties, who had been integrated into mainstream classrooms. The *sostegni* were given no further brief to work with mainstream pupils with less severe problems, or to pass on their training to other staff. They were to concentrate on the integration of their individual pupils.

At the same time, in the Quebec province of Canada, there were ambitious programmes of teacher INSET on both reading across the curriculum and integration (Csapo and Goguen, 1980). Teachers who were themselves undertaking Masters' degrees in special education helped university departments to carry out retraining programmes. As a result, large numbers of mainstream subject teachers had a chance to attend university-based special education courses and update their teaching skills.

DISCUSSION OF THE ORIGINAL DEFINITION

In Britain, by contrast, the impetus for reform had to come from the practitioners themselves. In a number of seminars, run by myself through Master's, Diploma and non-accredited courses in the North-East of England, mainstream special education teachers were asked to keep a diary of what they did, then to analyse the results by role and function and compare the results. These data were then compared with a contemporary matrix of role descriptors for SEN staff (Wilcox and Eustace, 1980). Nothing on the matrix fitted the realities of emerging post-Warnock good practice, so a new role had to be created.

The first thing that became clear was that if the government was unwilling to fund large-scale retraining, either by putting every individual teacher on a special education course or by asking universities to cascade the programmes, the Special Education Coordinator had to initiate it. The Coordinator was to 'fulfil a critical role ... developing staff expertise ... across the curriculum' (Sewell, 1982). From this, it followed that Coordinators differed from other middle managers in schools. They often had little status or formal power. If they called staff meetings to discuss the Warnock Report, few colleagues came along. What they did possess was a moral influence, based on their expertise with pupils with whom few colleagues seemed able to succeed. If they were to be agents of change, they had to be able to influence more staff. They had to be more than expert teachers, available to colleagues for consultation. They had to work with small groups of sympathetic teachers. The Coordinators had to have something of the ambition and influence of senior managers, bringing about change for the school as a whole, and effecting a more inclusive ethos.

What also made the role different from that of other middle managers – and continues to do so (Pickup, 1995) – was that it had to be grounded on the role of the pupil advocate, someone who would listen to and record the pupils' perspectives and use their voices to extend reform and evaluate its effectiveness. The small groups of special needs teachers from the North-East of England who came together with myself in 1981 to voice their concerns about the Warnock Report mapped out six major aspects to the role:

- to train mainstream subject teachers in the teaching of reading
- to extend the understanding of English across the curriculum
- to extend the attainments of slow learners in maths
- to involve subject staff in supporting pupils with special needs in their own subjects

- to enable more pupils with sensory, physical, behavioural and learning difficulties to integrate into mainstream classes
- to support the staff who 'reach out forcefully and successfully' to these pupils, as the pupils themselves saw it.

REFLECTION

- How does the job description of the person responsible for coordinating SEN provision in your school differ from this original definition?

FEEDBACK

The central issue for those who helped draw up that first definition of coordinated provision was the one that continues to disturb most mainstream staff: the teaching of reading (Lingard, 1994). There have been debates about the effectiveness of special classes for poor readers ever since they began. It had been clear since Collins' 1948 study (Collins, 1961) of remedial reading classes in primary schools that teaching poor readers the reading sub-skills in small groups with expert remedial teachers – and then returning them to the teachers who had originally failed them – produced short-term gains but no long-term improvement. In the years before Warnock, the Bullock Committee (1975), which had been set up to examine falling reading standards, thoroughly investigated Collins' findings and re-emphasized their importance. Those in favour of a coordinated staffing and training strategy for special needs provision argued that if schools accepted that teaching all pupils to read was the responsibility of every single member of staff – no matter what their subject – and that if sufficient numbers of mainstream teachers were trained in reading tuition, the pupils would continue to make gains in the long term. This would provide a starting point for the reshaping of special provision.

These findings appear to have been lost on both the Warnock Committee and the National Curriculum Council. The NCC English document makes no mention of 'reading recovery'. It limits the teaching of reading sub-skills to Level 2 in Key Stage 1. It seems to imply that pupils with reading difficulties will be enabled to cope with the demands of reading in a 'broad, balanced curriculum' with in-class support, and that it is unnecessary to teach the basic skills of reading at Key Stages 2, 3 or 4. Since the wider publicization of the work of Dame Marie Clay (1990) and the warnings about the numbers of adults with literacy problems from the Basic Skills Agency, the training of greater numbers of mainstream staff in the teaching of reading to pupils with special needs has moved up the agenda.

DISCUSSION OF THE FIRST ATTEMPTS AT COORDINATED PROVISION

Schools accepted the rationale for Special Needs Coordinators remarkably quickly. By 1984 virtually every primary school in Barnsley LEA (Ashcroft, 1986) had a Special Needs Coordinator in place. At first there was an increase in the Master's and Diploma courses to train Coordinators but as funding for teacher training was diverted from LEAs to schools in the late 1980s, this began to dry up. However, one or two of the early surveys found that many postholders were ill-equipped to carry it out, that the pace of integration was slowing and the attainments of pupils with learning difficulties had not risen. Even after the passing of the 1981 Education Act, designed to implement the Warnock Report, the proportion of pupils in special schools continued to rise, in contrast to most other parts of the Western world (Swann, 1985).

The early critics found that where the coordination of special provision was not working, it was because the Coordinators still thought of themselves as remedial teachers (Thomas and Feiler, 1988). They did not enjoy working alongside mainstream colleagues, supporting pupils in an integrated situation, and they were fatalistic about the ethos of their schools. They preferred to take children out of mainstream classrooms and offer them teaching that bore little relation to mainstream programmes of study. They identified pupils for special provision with norm referenced tests (which bore little relation to the work they were actually doing), teacher recommendation (which often led to the over-representation of pupils with behavioural difficulties), and questionable prior records. When these former remedial teachers did attempt support teaching with pupils with special needs in mainstream classes, the pupils felt embarrassed and labelled (Bines, 1986).

Unused to a management role, some of these early SEN Coordinators gave themselves insufficient time to plan team teaching. They did not accept the importance of whole-school inservice training. The planning of some of the early support teaching was also reactive rather than proactive. The Coordinators tended to start with teachers' needs (particularly the teachers with the greatest discipline problems) rather than with the pupils' learning abilities or perspectives. The issues of how to raise the awareness of more mainstream teachers, of involving a greater number of them in the practicalities of special provision, of motivating them to adopt more effective teaching and disciplinary practices (Bell and Best, 1988) had hardly been addressed – by the Coordinators, their senior managers or heads. Overall, few coordinators seemed to have had much effect on the achievements or expectations of pupils. Even before the Baker

Reform Bill was published, the dream of coordinated special provision based on 'every teacher a teacher of Special Needs' (Booth *et al.*, 1987) seemed as far off as ever.

REFLECTIONS ON CURRENT PRACTICE IN YOUR SCHOOL

- When was the role of SEN Coordinator formalized in your school?
- How much time does the Coordinator spend:

  - withdrawing pupils?
  - team teaching?
  - in joint planning?
  - on INSET?
  - with outside agencies?
  - with parents?

- How are SEN pupils identified in your school?
- How does your school track attainment trends in SEN pupils?

FEEDBACK

The 1991 HMI survey of special provision found 'significant shortfalls ... in clear statements of policy, in ... planning, management and ... systematic evaluation'. They noted 'much goodwill' but emphasized that more progress needed to be made in 'assessing pupils' capabilities in curricular terms'. Overall they declared that the special needs sector was 'not well prepared to meet the challenges of the 1990s' – in other words, the introduction of the National Curriculum and its assessment procedures and the devolution of resource management to school and middle management levels.

DISCUSSION: ERA AND ITS IMPLICATIONS

By the time the Education Reform Bill was enacted, there was considerable disillusionment with the Warnock Report and special provision in mainstream schools. 'Investment in success' was the new watchword; the National Curriculum, league tables and parental choice were supposed to 'lever up' the attainments of all mainstream pupils. The government would protect the 2 to 3 per cent with statements of special needs, most of whom were still in special schools, but for the 18 per cent in mainstream schools there was thought to be little need for additional resourcing (Pumfrey and Mittler, 1989).

If, as the National Curriculum Council had originally argued, every child was to have an 'individual curriculum plan', the government argued that this would inevitably lead to the differentiation of teaching for all, including those with mild learning and behavioural difficulties. Schools were to respond to market forces and if they failed to 'lever up' the achievements of pupils – able and less able – they would lose income and eventually either change or close.

Hard-nosed critics of special education also asked how Warnock concepts, like the modified and developmental curriculum, could fit into the National Curriculum. If all pupils had to follow all ten subjects of the 'broad, balanced curriculum' plus RE, no one subject had any higher claim for special needs support. Since it was plainly impractical to provide SEN support for every department all of the time, it would arguably be more appropriate for heads to replace mainstream special needs staff with National Curriculum subject specialists. Schools in the survey recorded the loss of some special needs teachers, and specialist teaching materials, but we still have little understanding of the amount of special needs resources which were redirected away from the most vulnerable groups of children by heads and governors in this period.

REFLECTIONS

- How far did your school move towards individual curriculum plans for all pupils?
- How many special needs teachers did your school have before ERA?
- Have the principles on which SEN time and resources are allocated been included in your SEN policy?

FEEDBACK

The notion that all pupils should have individual curriculum plans met with considerable opposition from the profession. The first draft of the Code suggested that pupils at Key Stage 1 of the SEN identification and assessment procedures should have an individual education plan, but after consultation this was limited to the much smaller groups of pupils at Stage 2. Among the survey schools, it has become the responsibility of the form teacher to record 'action plans' for pupils at Stage 1. Hornby *et al*. (1995) call these additional help proformas. Individual education plans are reserved for Stages 2 and 3.

As Schedule II of the Statutory Instruments No. 1048 (DfE, 1994b) makes clear, all governing bodies must henceforth provide information on the way that resources which are devolved from LEAs for special needs and additional needs are actually allocated. Among the survey schools, this was having a marked effect on SEN planning and the implementation of the Code. As one teacher commented, 'Now we know we have to be accountable for SEN funding, we have to be seen to be spending it on SEN provision'.

DISCUSSION: CONSOLIDATING COORDINATED PROVISION

However great the ideological pressure, the government never entirely abandoned the Warnock notion that 20 per cent of pupils had special needs. It was written into all of the National Curriculum documents. *A Curriculum for All* (NCC, 1989) accepted that there was an estimated '20 per cent of pupils with SEN'. Though government reforms apparently made integration harder, it was clear by the time of the joint HMI and Audit Commission Report (DES, 1992) that segregation of the 2–3 per cent with statements was indefensible – in terms of expense and effectiveness as well as of parental choice.

The 1993 OFSTED Report on *Access and Achievement in Urban Schools* also made clear that the tide of reform was leaving as many as 20 per cent of schools 'stranded'. Pupils in urban areas with 'particular needs', i.e. the most able and those with learning difficulties, were seen as particularly vulnerable. Parental choice and the National Curriculum had not raised standards in areas of deprivation – and this was arguably interpreted by the DfE as a warning about the standards of the Warnock 20 per cent in all schools.

So the *Code of Practice on the Identification and Assessment of Special Educational Needs* which enshrines the role of Coordinator offers something more than a restatement of existing principles. Professor Klaus Wedell (1993) suggested that the first draft came as a response to concern about the 1993 Education Act by and on behalf of parents, voluntary organizations and SEN teachers. It is probably also true that, like the 1993/94 Dearing Reports on the National Curriculum, it represents part of a wider move by the government away from confrontation over issues of educational assessment towards consultation and consolidation.

The Code re-emphasizes the government's commitment to the Warnock notion that special provision is to be seen as a continuum. Twenty per cent of the population may have special needs at some time in their schooling – not just the 2–3 per cent who have statements: and the levels of support needed will vary from child to child. This commitment is to be delivered through the governing bodies of schools in the first instance. They are to be responsible for determining a school's SEN policy. Special provision is to be managed by the headteacher. It is to be monitored by the LEA and OFSTED. Responsibility for the 'operation' of the SEN policy will rest with the SEN Coordinator or team. And it is all to be grounded on what the Code refers to as 'expressions of concern' by class teachers, external agencies and parents.

REFLECTIONS

- Has the way in which resources are allocated to and among pupils with SEN been published in your school?
- How are these pupils' needs identified and reviewed?
- What are the arrangements for providing them with access to the National Curriculum?
- How are they integrated in your school?
- What specialist SEN resources and accommodation are available?
- Which of your governors has a special interest in SEN issues?
- How do they deal with complaints about SEN issues?
- When did your governors last review SEN policy and practice?
- How confident are the staff in your school about identifying the special needs of their pupils?

FEEDBACK

Most schools already have fairly comprehensive SEN policies (Landy, 1994). Formal responsibility for the production of an SEN policy and an annual report on special needs are laid on the governing body – though in most schools these will be drafted by the Special Needs Coordinators. The main aspects of the policy statement are laid down in the 1993 Education Act and Circular 6/94 on the organization of special educational provision. The guidelines for a policy statement also form part of the OFSTED framework (Chorley, 1993). There is little that is new or surprising in these guidelines and inservice work to enable schools to update their policies is not difficult to arrange.

MANAGEMENT TASK: DRAFTING AN SEN POLICY

Review your existing SEN policy document. The following guidelines, based on Circular 6/94, might prove useful:

- the general principles of SEN provision in your school
- the principles by which the school's funds are allocated to SEN

- the name of the SENCo
- levels and kinds of support
- special facilities, accommodation and resources
- any additional admission procedures for pupils with SEN
- identification of SEN pupils and assessment procedures
- integration arrangements
- curriculum

  - access to National Curriculum
  - modifications and exceptions to NC
  - differentiation
  - individual education plans

- SEN INSET
- links with external agencies, other schools and colleges
- evaluation and complaints procedures.

FEEDBACK

Since the publication of the 1993 Education Act, it has become relatively easy to identify what kind of issues to address in a policy document. The survey schools often included a 'vision statement', as well as notice of how SEN provision fits into the school's budget plan. A professional development day spent revising the policy can ensure that everyone will know who is responsible for coordinating special provision and what kinds of special facilities and accommodation are available. It can also help to bring about agreement on the long-term planning of SEN inservice training, so that all the staff feel they have 'ownership' of the programme (Harvey, 1995).

DISCUSSION OF CURRENT CONCERNS

When Mary Warnock chaired the Committee of Enquiry into the education of handicapped children and young people, the role of the SEN coordinator had not been created. She has since argued (Warnock, 1994) that there is no need for SENCos in many schools, just that there should be a few 'experts on the staff to whom others may turn for immediate support'. This is all that is necessary in her view for a school to achieve a 'whole-school policy'. In some schools, it is true, special provision became such a low-status, undeveloped area in the 1980s that the only staff who now feel any commitment to special needs issues are a part-time coordinator and a few poorly trained 'link teachers' from subject departments.

With the introduction of the National Curriculum, the old remedial groups may have gone, but some heads have replaced them with bottom-stream classes. These contain rather more pupils than the old remedial classes. Many of their pupils have untreated learning difficulties in the 'three Rs'. They are selected on the basis of questionable prior records and teacher recommendation and the class may become a 'sink' for pupils with behavioural difficulties. There may also be more amenable pupils with learning difficulties in the higher streams, but these pupils' needs may be overlooked. The problem with Mary Warnock's argument is that in such a context, the few 'experts' and 'link staff' merely have a de-skilling effect on the rest of the teachers. They take responsibility for the children in the bottom streams away from the rest of the staff, rather than raising the awareness of special needs among the staff as a whole. Labels are reinforced and the 'context of failure' is confirmed.

REFLECTIONS

- How many staff belong to the special needs or learning support team of your school?
- How has this changed since the 1980s?
- How many other staff teach classes which contain pupils with special needs?

FEEDBACK

In many of the survey schools, despite all the problems of the late 1980s, the Coordinator has often given a focus to the school's most deeply cherished ideas. In all the primary schools and one of the secondary schools, the Coordinator brought together and trained voluntary groups of well-inclined parents to teach reading and to support individual pupils with particular needs. The volunteers had not supplanted staff support, but extended it. In some of the secondary schools, special needs provision is so managed that members of the mainstream staff receive some training in SEN assessment and provision and asssume responsibility for small groups of pupils with special needs. In some of these schools, special provision is grounded on a cyclical, school-based, inservice programme, which allows *ad hoc* groups of teachers the experience of acting in a withdrawal and support role.

This inservice role is now more important than ever, given the government's reluctance to fund a national training programme for all mainstream staff (Mittler, 1994). It is this inservice training, underpinned by the experience of withdrawal and support work, that gives the mainstream subject staff of these schools the confidence to articulate their concerns about pupils' special needs. This strategy of involving a range of staff in providing and defining special provision ensures that practice and policy are clearly linked.

In this kind of inservice and staffing strategy, the Coordinator is much more than the 'SEN expert', the person who drafts the 'vision statement' and the rest of the SEN policy for the Governing Body, or who administers multi-staged SEN assessment and files the paperwork. The Coordinator listens to the staff and to the parents, and provides a practical focus for their most deeply felt concerns about both individual children and the whole-school context. As the remainder of this book makes clear, these whole-school concerns may cover a far wider range of pupils than was originally envisaged by the Warnock Committee. The Coordinator articulates a vision of what is possible, provides and arranges teacher training and returns responsibility to those who must exercise it – mainstream subject teachers, their pupils and the pupils' parents.

As the survey schools have found out, this process of practical policy-making cannot stop with the staff. It must also be extended to pupils, parents and governors. It may be possible for small special interest groups of staff, pupils, parents and governors to bring their particular concerns to the Coordinator in the drafting of the SEN policy's basic principles. Statemented pupils with mobility difficulties at Eastville School, for instance, met as a group and decided that the most important thing for them was that they should be allowed full access to out-of-school activities, residentials and school trips. Parents of statemented pupils also met and included a declaration that no decision about providing or withdrawing extra SEN support should be made without their full involvement.

A coordinated SEN staffing and training strategy ensures that all staff who teach the National Curriculum to SEN pupils are confident and experienced enough to write their own departmental policies on special provision. A clear set of general principles is not enough: the policy needs to correspond to teachers' working practices if it is to affect expectations and achievements.

The Code of Practice goes a long way towards recognizing this when it bases Stage 1 of the identification and assessment process on the classroom teachers' 'expressions of concern'. This vital phrase reminds us that the assessment process nearly always starts with the parent or classroom teacher – not the expert SENCo, the psychologist or the doctor – and that if pupils with special needs are to raise their expectations and attainments significantly, they will need an increasing proportion of staff who can reach out 'forcefully and effectively' to them.

PUPIL PERSPECTIVES

Most schools now invite their pupils, including those with special needs, to include self-critical comments as part of their annual profile. However, it is relatively rare for schools to listen to pupils' comments on the quality of their learning experience or the school's management structure. This is seen as a delicate issue, especially when it touches on pupils with special needs. However, many teachers have found that where there is a concerted attempt to raise the self-esteem and confidence of all pupils and where pupils are listened to with tact and sensitivity, these comments can provide those who maintain the trust of both pupils and colleagues an invaluable addition to the range of evaluation strategies.

In the decade since the notion of Special Needs Coordinator was conceived, I have collected unsolicited comments about the role from pupils with no special needs, from non-statemented mainstream pupils with special needs and from those with statements. For most pupils, the SENCo appears to be 'just another teacher'. There may be something unusual in that he or she teaches 'reading', English and maths. The specific focus may well be seen as educating 'people who need help', helping people with 'special needs get a better education and jobs' or 'looking after people like us'. In some schools, the SENCo is also seen as 'head of discipline', dealing with 'naughty pupils' and 'making sure we're good', though this aspect of the role would be missing in many others. In other schools, pupils understand that the SENCo works with gifted pupils and truants as well.

Pupils in schools with coordinated SEN staffing strategies may well be aware that the SENCo has to 'talk to people – parents, teachers and governors' – and to 'teach teachers'. Where this is so, pupils want to be reassured that a SENCo does not talk about them behind their backs. However, there are other pupils and their parents who feel that as soon as the SENCo hears about their difficulties, all staff should know and understand. These pupils and parents expect much higher levels of staff communication and they can be much more critical if important information is not digested or acted on by the staff as a whole.

SUMMARY

In retrospect, the lack of government vision and commitment to the integration of pupils with disabilities and learning difficulties into mainstream schools and to the raising of expectations has become even clearer since the Warnock Report was published. Teacher training resources for special provision were cut back in the late

1980s and 1990s; in the aftermath of the Education Reform Act, the resources of mainstream schools were diverted away from special provision – just in what quantities is still unclear. In many schools, SEN Coordinators were given an extraordinary difficult role, for which they were only partly prepared. In some schools, it even became a part-time job, involving a large class teaching commitment with little opportunity to develop its managerial and inservice aspects.

In the wake of the publication of its Code of Practice, the government has once again shown little commitment to the large-scale retraining of classroom teachers. It would seem that if changes are to occur, they will have to come from within the schools and be led by the Coordinators. These now have a responsibility for the day-to-day operations of whole-school SEN policies, including the crucial ones of INSET and staff development. If the identification and assessment of pupils with special needs are to be effectively managed, time will have to be set aside to allow the Coordinator to listen to what the Code refers to as the 'expressions of concern' of classroom teachers. These are to become the basis for the first stage of the identification process.

In schools which operate a Coordinated SEN staffing strategy, training members of the mainstream staff to become involved in withdrawal and support work can ensure that these 'concerns' are based on experience. These concerns can also provide a focus for a school's most cherished ideals which, effectively harnessed, can make a difference to the integration, expectations and attainments of pupils with special needs.

2

School-based assessment

INTRODUCTION

Between the publication of the Education Reform Bill (DES, 1986) and that of the 1993 Draft Code of Practice, there was considerable confusion about the role of special educators in the assessment of non-statemented pupils. Previously, most Special Needs Coordinators had used standardized IQ, reading, spelling and maths tests to screen out pupils with special needs and to provide colleagues with diagnostic information about deficits in basic skills. With the introduction of National Curriculum assessments, the old norm referenced tests appeared redundant. As originally conceived, SATs and Teacher Assessments seemed to be much more closely related to what the teachers were actually teaching; they could be administered by the children's teachers, and they offered detailed, diagnostic evidence of what the pupils were learning.

When the early SATs were slimmed down, however, they lost much of the diagnostic element (TES, 1995). Some SEN Coordinators also felt they were less precise and reliable than the old norm referenced tests. Some LEA advisers worried that different schools were defining special needs in different ways, while the Audit Commission were concerned about inconsistencies within and between LEAs.

In many schools, SEN assessment had come to comprise a mixture of National Curriculum assessments, norm referenced tests and the staged assessment procedures outlined in the Warnock Report (DES, 1978). These had become particularly highly developed in the case of emotional and behavioural difficulties. Some secondary schools had sophisticated multi-stage behavioural management structures, involving incident slips for the most basic forms of disruptive behaviour, referral slips, green, yellow and red report forms in ascending degrees of seriousness, meetings with parents, referrals to outside agencies, meetings with governors, and final warnings. At a time of rapidly changing family structures and employment patterns, these multi-staged pupil management structures allowed schools to monitor all their difficult pupils with a minimum of paperwork. The main problems with these schemes were that they were reactive rather than proactive, and that they were applied differently in different schools. The Code of Practice confirmed the role of special educators in schools' assessment procedures. It put curricular planning at the heart of special educational provision and offered SENCos a new opportunity to involve their colleagues in planned inservice. It consolidated the links between assessment in the National Curriculum and the more traditional screening and diagnostic procedures. Furthermore, many aspects of the Code were to be familiar to schools and LEAs which implemented the recommendations of the Warnock Report. As Hornby *et al*. (1995) put it, 'The Code . . . provides the most far reaching guidance on this subject ever aimed at teachers in mainstream schools'. The underlying principles of the Code could be summarized as:

- early, quick and thorough identification and assessment
- effective record keeping
- liaison with outside agencies
- the education of pupils with special needs alongside mainstream peers, 'whenever appropriate'
- partnership with parents
- pupil consultation as appropriate to age and understanding.

The Code could easily have faced rejection in schools, however, because of the amount of time and bureaucracy it seemed to involve. Some key phrasing – especially that which relates to the thresholds between the various stages – is ambiguous and difficult to interpret. It does not include all the groups of pupils whose needs teachers are most concerned about. Among the schools that took part in the survey, however, there was a willingness to simplify the paperwork, to adapt it to existing procedures where these benefited the pupils with special needs and the school, to include additional groups of pupils to those defined by Warnock as having special needs and to accept the role of moderation as a way of developing consensus and consistency between schools.

Like the National Curriculum, the Code appears to lack a coherent educational philosophy for children with special needs. It seems to offer strategies rather than an orientation. What came through from the survey schools was that they saw the assessment of special needs as fitting into a wider value system, which embraced teachers as well as pupils. This had enabled these schools to promote their special educational provision without forfeiting local community support through the early 1990s.

OBJECTIVES

By the end of this chapter, you will be able to:

- relate the structure of the new Code to the underlying Warnock recommendations
- review your current identification and assessment processes
- review the role of school contexts
- review the place of parental and pupil views
- produce an individual education plan.

DISCUSSION OF THE WARNOCK MODEL

The establishment of staged assessment through the Code of Practice has been portrayed as both new and daunting, especially in media accounts of teacher union reaction. Union Secretaries (e.g. McAvoy, 1994) have made clear that they are not opposed to the Code. What they want is a slimming down of the paperwork, more training for SEN Coordinators and classroom teachers and more time for them to consult each other. In schools which operated Warnock styles of assessment, staged assessment is part of the warp and weft of everyday working practice. The progress of pupils with SEN is discussed as part of the regular cycle of meetings between SEN and pastoral staff, outside agencies, pupils and parents. Differentiation and modifications to programmes of study are regularly on the agenda of curriculum development meetings. Annual reviews and transition planning are tied into profiling and there are regular, planned consultations between school staff, pupils and parents.

The five-stage model in the Code is clearly based on Warnock. The Committee had envisaged that the first three stages of SEN assessment should be school-based. In the first instance, the class or form teacher would consult the headteacher, who would then be responsible for marshalling all the relevant information from the child's file, from medical and 'social' sources and, 'where possible', from the parents. Progress would be monitored and detailed records kept in the child's file. At this stage there would be no separate or additional forms to fill in and no additional special needs plan.

The second stage involved a 'teacher with training and expertise in special education' – either a member of staff or a local advisory teacher, since the role of SEN Coordinator had not yet been defined. 'The prescription of a special programme' would be delayed until Stage 2. This would be supervised at the school by the 'specialist', but again there would be no separate special needs paperwork. It was not until the third stage that the headteacher or the school doctor would consider calling in outside agencies like the local peripatetic teachers for sensory impairment, the psychologist, Social Services or health workers.

Stages 4 and 5 involved the multi-disciplinary assessment that many of Warnock's commentators saw as the most distinctive contribution of the Committee. The use of specially devised special education forms was to be reserved until Stage 4. Reviews of children at Stages 1–3 were to be based on records of progress in the pupil's folder, supplemented by test scores and checklists. Warnock suggested that 'These should be simple and easy to apply' (4.52).

Appendix 3 of the Warnock Report outlines a 'possible grid', which combined descriptors of need with prescriptions of placement. The grid includes sensory, physical, language, emotional and behavioural, intellectual and specific learning difficulties which it then categorizes as 'no impairment', 'slight', 'moderate', 'severe' and 'total'. Prescriptions vary from special help in ordinary class, to inclusion in a special class or unit in an ordinary school, to placement in a special school. The Warnock Committee argued that it would be 'essential' to provide schools with more detailed definitions and guidance and to carry out a feasibility study of the grid, though they did not include these suggestions in their findings.

REFLECTIONS

- How many of the Warnock proposals were built into your school's assessment procedures?
- Have you used special education forms for school-based assessments?

DISCUSSION OF STAGE 1

As part of their contracted 1265 hours, most schools already hold regular meetings for subject and class teachers to raise their concerns about the progress and pastoral needs of their pupils. In a few of the survey schools, including one of the secondaries, this was carried out at a regular whole-staff meeting. In most of the primary schools, there were special meetings between the SENCo and the reception, Key Stage 1 and Key Stage 2 teams (Harvey, 1995). In most secondary schools, discussion of individual pupils was devolved to year or other pastoral groups.

Many schools, including most of those in the survey group, also carry out half-termly, simple, written checks on progress in all National Curriculum subjects, progress in basic skills, attitude, behaviour and attendance – in addition to termly reports to parents and the full annual profiling. These informal checks can be timed to fit into the pattern of Stage 1 SEN meetings, so that discussions can be based on up to date evidence from across the curriculum. These reports can be set out as a computerized checklist, requiring something as easy to complete as A/B/C grades for progress in class, for attitude, behaviour and attendance, but they provide a regular channel of communication within the primary team – or between the secondary form tutor and subject teachers – and between the school, the pupils and their parents. This pattern of meetings and written checks can very easily be adapted to provide a forum for the 'expressions of concern' that underpin Stage 1 of the Code. Without them, it can often be difficult for the SEN Coordinator to hear the concerns of classroom teachers.

REFLECTIONS

- What are the arrangements in your school for form or subject teachers to express their concerns to the SEN Coordinator?
- What opportunities are there for staff to record their concerns?
- Are there opportunities for class and subject teachers to discuss their pupils' special needs with outside agencies?
- How often can staff meet parents to discuss their concerns, and verify or update SEN records?

FEEDBACK

As a management goal, it is probably helpful to fit Stage 1 meetings with the SEN team into a pre-existing pattern of team meetings. In inner city or urban comprehensives with large numbers of statemented pupils and non-statemented pupils with special needs, the only way to ensure that all these pupils are carefully monitored is to pre-plan a cycle of meetings between all the tutors from one year group, the year tutor and a member of the SEN team. Wherever possible, Stage 1 records can be reduced to computerized checklists with simple action plans. These can be translated into *D*own to earth, *A*chievable, *R*ealistic and *T*ime-constrained (DARTs) targets for the pupils.

As this cycle of meetings can involve the whole staff, there should be a clear division of responsibilities. This is the pattern that Eastville, a secondary survey school, followed:

- It is the subject teacher's responsibility to marshal information about effort and progress for all the pupils in his or her classes once a term.

- It is the form teacher's responsibility to gather information on behaviour and attendance.
- It is the year tutor's responsibility to decide the point at which the school is to notify parents, seek the child's views, review assessment records and contact the first layer of external services.
- It is the SEN team's responsibility to pass on diagnostic details from tests or information from outside agencies like GPs, Social Services or Education Social Worker.

THE TRIGGER

According to the Code of Practice, the 'trigger' for Stage 1 is an 'expression of concern'. These terms are probably the most distinctive features of the new Code. The notion of a 'concern' had a particular resonance for so many of the survey teachers and their SENCos. During the turbulent period between the late 1980s and 1994, when the National Curriculum tests were being introduced and then constantly revised and so few staff had a clear idea of the role of special education in school-based assessments, it was their 'concern' about the marginalization of pupils with low attainments, with emotional or behavioural difficulties or simply with the growing number of poor families, that enabled so many of the survey schools to retain their sense of community, unity and direction.

According to the Code, any teacher or other professional or the pupil's parent can raise a 'concern', though it would normally be 'expressed to or by the child's class teacher in a primary school or form or year tutor in a secondary school'.

There was keen debate among the survey schools about how easily pupils should be allowed to go on to the Stage 1 list. Some teachers, who were using separate registration forms and requiring parents to sign these before a child could join Stage 1, were finding the procedures extremely time consuming. They had a systemic motive for wanting to draw the definition of a 'concern' as tightly as possible. Other teachers argued that even to place pupils on a Stage 1 register for half a term could label them and unwittingly lower their teachers' or their parents' expectations. There had been no large-scale training programme for mainstream staff in how to identify and assess special needs, and staff could add names to a checklist for all kinds of reasons. They had an ethical motive for wanting to limit the numbers at Stage 1.

Other schools disagreed strongly. They felt that it would be unwise for individual heads or SENCos to be too prescriptive about what can act as a 'trigger' for Stage 1 identification and assessment. It might well have shown rather more vision for the government to have initiated a whole-scale retraining programme for class and subject teachers to help them understand the principles of special needs assessment (Mittler, 1994). But if none was forthcoming, it would be up to the SENCo to plan a school-based inservice programme, embracing all the stages in SEN assessment. They argued that at this very early stage of the assessment procedure, teachers' experience and common sense should be trusted. The problems about completing proformas and gathering signatures should not be allowed to prevent SENCos from establishing whole-school SEN assessment policies and practices. If necessary, the forms should be simplified to fit the policy and SEN consultations should be reserved for regular parents' meetings.

REFLECTIONS

- What are the main kinds of concerns raised in your school?
- Are there any concerns that do not fit easily into the Warnock model of 'special educational needs'?

FEEDBACK

Several of the survey schools regarded the Warnock definitions of learning difficulties as too restrictive a basis for Stage 1 assessment. The issue of 'gifted' pupils was specifically excluded from the Warnock Committee's discussions. In some schools, however, staff would want to use Stage 1 meetings to discuss this very important minority. Some of the urban and inner city schools also wanted to review pupils with attendance and lateness problems. Others even wanted to look at underachievers across the ability range.

One SENCo from a school in an affluent area felt that his most anxious parents were those with 'dyslexic' children. These pupils were articulate and bright. Their reading and spelling ages were only marginally less than their chronological ages and the discrepancy between their apparent IQ and their reading quotients was certainly much less than the two standard deviations commonly agreed on as signifying specific learning difficulties. This SENCo wanted to include these pupils on his Stage 1 register as a way of alerting staff to the parents' concerns. While uneasy about it, he felt that this use of labelling would not harm these children and diverted no resources away from other pupils whose special needs fitted Warnock definitions.

Schools with large numbers of poor readers, or with a high proportion of integrated statemented pupils or – like the school described above in the affluent area – with a positive vision of special education, may want to include rather more groups of pupils on their Stage 1 register than the Warnock definitions allow.

THE STAGE 1 REGISTER

The Code suggests that the class and subject teacher will gather information and make an 'initial assessment' of each child's special educational needs. It is their responsibility to provide special help from 'within the normal curriculum framework, exploring ways in which increased differentiation' might help. It is the SEN Coordinator's duty to ensure that the child is included on the SEN register.

REFLECTIONS

- Who is responsible for SEN record keeping in your school?
    - the SENCo
    - the Heads of Department
    - the pastoral post holders
    - the form tutors
    - the subject teachers
    - all of these staff?
- How does your school ensure that there is effective communication between subject staff, pupils, form teachers, subject departments, pastoral managers and the SEN team?
- How does your school ensure that SEN records are available to all the staff that come into contact with these pupils?

FEEDBACK

So as to involve the whole staff in the identification of pupils with SEN, some of the survey schools made it the responsibility of each of their class teachers to gather the information on progress within the National Curriculum and in the basic skills. Careful advance planning of the staff calendar could ensure that this information could be collected 'just in time' (Peters and Waterman, 1982) for the Stage 1 meeting. Concerns about attendance and behaviour were gathered by the form teacher in secondary schools. This was the evidence on which the Stage 1 register was drawn up. Information on medical or sensory problems could be added to the register from the main school databases. The form tutor would set targets for the pupil –

some as simple as wearing glasses, or staying seated all lesson, or doing 20 minutes' reading practice every night at home. These targets could then be circulated to the subject staff. At Eastville School, the pupils were given a DARTs target card, with an attractive 'Bull's Eye' logo and space for the form teacher to write three targets on the front – and a timetable on the back for teachers to 'score' how well that pupil had met the targets in each lesson.

At Southville School, so as to minimize paperwork, this Stage 1 register simply comprised a class list taken from the school's central computer, overprinted with a ticklist, space for brief action plans and a list of review dates. The ticklist contained all the Warnock categories of 'special educational needs' but it also included a range of problems that are recurrent in that school and about which their staff frequently express concern, including:

- reading difficulties
- oracy
- writing difficulties
- problems in the wider curriculum
- health and physical problems
- sensory impairment
- behavioural difficulties
- attendance.

In an urban comprehensive like Eastville, which also mentioned attendance, the more able and talented and statemented pupils on its ticklist, and where as many as 60 per cent of its pupils had particular needs at some time in their schooling, it was considered important that none was overlooked. Eastville staff were particularly anxious about underachievement among the very few very able pupils.

After the Stage 1 meeting at Eastville, it became the form tutors' responsibility to ensure that the Stage 1 DARTs target cards were shown to all the subject teachers by the pupils. Lists of pupils with reading, writing, oracy, maths, sensory or health difficulties were circulated by the SENCo and could easily be added to mark-books. This gave subject teachers the opportunity to set their own objectives for differentiation and support. The set of Stage 1 SEN form registers was kept in a SEN file by the year tutor. Also contained in the year tutor's file was a set of other year lists, including:

- intake pupils' reading and maths scores
- SATs scores
- Year 11 anticipated GCSE scores
- pupils with health or sensory difficulties
- pupils with SEN statements
- attendance problems.

DISCUSSION OF THE REVIEW PROCESS

The Code suggests that the progress of pupils at Stage 1 is reviewed every term or at least every six months. It is essential that this is done and seen to be done, given the possibility that any child with special needs may progress to Stages 3 and 4, or that the parents may decide they want to appeal against a school or LEA decision and take the matter to a SEN Tribunal.

The Code also suggests that information collected at Stage 1 will reveal 'different perceptions of those concerned with the child'. Where schools are already able to assess whole-class or even whole-school populations, SEN reviews can also be carried out more regularly.

REFLECTION

• How frequently does your school review pupils at Stage 1?

FEEDBACK

At Eastville School, the pupils on the Stage 1 registers are reviewed twice each term. Registers, circulated among all who attend, subject staff and the senior management team, keep staff up to date about pupils who are presenting the school with concerns at minimal cost in terms of paperwork. Other schools in the LEA had instigated a computerized database using technical assistance, but the survey schools preferred to keep their data-gathering close to the class teachers. They also felt that the computer database would be too time-consuming to maintain. Their prime SEN management aims were to develop good communications and to minimize the chances of overloading staff.

DISCUSSION OF THE ROLE OF SCHOOL CONTEXTS

One of the suggestions outlined in the 1993 Draft Code was that pupils at Stage 1 should have an individual education plan. The idea was dropped when the 1994 Code of Practice was published and the staff in the survey schools certainly felt this to be sensible. The prospect of large urban secondary schools having to complete formal curricular plans for 200 to 300 pupils with special needs and to review and update them every term was daunting. Brief action plans outlining kinds of support and making short references to existing good practice in the school can help build on and enhance good cross-curricular developments. In any case, the survey schools were finding that most of the pupils reported for Stage 1 discussion had mild learning or behavioural difficulties, and it is arguable that most of these mild difficulties are both ephemeral and context related.

A child who is having mild problems in one area of the curriculum may be doing relatively well in another. Progress can be made through differentiated teaching styles or through effective classroom management. Similarly, pupils doing badly at one stage of their school careers may do comparatively well at others. Two of the survey schools, Eastville and Southville, analysed the achievements of pupils who arrived at their schools with reading difficulties and compared them with leaving grades at GCSE. They found very little correlation between them at the level of individual pupil scores.

The survey schools were confident that these regular short-term checks on effort, progress, attendance and behaviour did have an effect on overall achievement in the long term, however. The South-ville SENCo commented that 'It is essential that Coordinators make colleagues feel that they are being listened to'. There is a sense that the 'expression of concerns' helps promote a unity of purpose. That SENCo would argue that it is when staff believe someone from the SEN team is listening to their concerns, that the class teachers are most likely to 'alter their teaching strategies'. Listening to colleagues may also convince staff that effective SEN provision depends on a pooling of expertise, a 'sharing of ideas' – that 'every teacher is a teacher of special needs'.

In order to involve staff in SEN identification and assessment procedures, most SENCos in the survey schools asked colleagues to take part in evidence gathering. In junior and secondary schools, form or subject teachers set and marked literacy screening tests. Most of the maths coordinators and heads of department surveyed had decided on their own screening tests. Time was set aside in most of the secondary schools, so that every maths, science and English teacher could read and update National Curriculum profiles in their subjects from the sending school. In the primary schools surveyed, all reception and Key Stage 1 staff were invited to implement and use an infants' rating scale. The most up to date of these, for example, Martin Desforges and Geoff Lindsay's *Infants Index* (1995), include National Curriculum criteria. They are norm referenced and are scored to indicate the stage in the Code of Practice at which pupils can be placed. In most survey schools, staff have completed annual profiles and Records of Achievement for pupils with special needs and have consulted these pupils in the process.

The Warnock pattern of SEN assessment seemed to suggest a hierarchy of professional expertise, with specialist prescription and advice reserved for the later stages. But there is no reason why the school nurse, the Education Social Worker and the Educational Psychologist should not attend the Stage 1 meetings from time to time, so that staff who work most closely with the children can raise issues which concern them directly. Indeed, occasional pre-planned Stage 1 meetings, with this wider range of professionals, can generate considerable commitment on all sides.

REFLECTIONS

- How quickly can the teachers in your school get to know about changes in the health status, behaviour and attainments of pupils with SEN?
- Is there any opportunity for your class teachers to meet members of outside agencies?
- How appropriate is the information in the school files of your pupils with SEN one year later?

FEEDBACK

Eastville School had a calendar of meetings which ensured that the nurse, the Education Social Worker and the Educational Psychologist each attended at least one Stage 1 meeting every year, as part of their SEN preventive strategy.

SCHOOL CONTEXTS AND CROSS-PHASE ASSESSMENT

It is now becoming a matter of routine for many schools and colleges to be involved in cross-phase reviews of statemented pupils long before transfer. Secondary special needs teams often attend the transitional SEN reviews from the sending primary schools and FE special needs staff the transitional planning meetings in the secondaries. They collate all the data on the registers and individual statements, summarize them and verify the information through talking to parents. This liaison pattern is also being extended to mainstream pupils on the first three stages of SEN assessment. For both statemented and non-statemented pupils with SEN, data can quickly become out of date and misleading. Many learning or behavioural difficulties turn out to be contextual.

REFLECTION

- Are there pupils in your school whose difficulties have turned out to be either much less or much more severe than the sending school suggested?

FEEDBACK

At Eastville School, there were two cousins with markedly similar language and learning difficulties who had been to different primary schools. The one with arguably the more troubled childhood had been assessed in school and given school-based special provision suitable for children with mild reading difficulties; the other had been assessed by outside agencies, given the protection of a statement and support from LEA teachers for those with specific learning difficulties, for those with emotional and behavioural difficulties, and speech therapy.

Another pupil, with a degenerative physical condition and described on his statement as having severe language and learning difficulties, had never spoken at his primary school, yet appeared to be relatively fluent at home. One term after transfer to the comprehensive, he was beginning to use complex sentences in school. It would seem essential for those who have to use the information to check it out thoroughly.

PARTNERSHIP WITH PARENTS AND OUTSIDE AGENCIES

At some of the survey schools, a data summary is drawn up by staff from both the sending and receiving schools, then checked with parents, the school nurse and other paramedics before it is passed on to the teachers. At Eastville, following the annual profiling and review season, there are audits of need with the paramedics and each of their line managers. This is so that medical and paramedic interventions can be fitted into the timetable for the following year and so that the health personnel have up to date records for their managers.

REFLECTIONS

- How much prior information does your school receive about SEN?
- How closely are your staff involved in screening procedures?
- How much information do you pass on to the next sector?
- How much opportunity do parents get to check SEN data?
- How closely are the pupils consulted?

DISCUSSION OF STAGE 2

The Code argues that some schools will want to combine Stages 1 and 2 of the Code. This certainly made sense to the SENCos of some of the survey primary schools, particularly in relation to pupils in reception and Key Stage 1. Most of the serious problems would be discussed and acted on at Stage 1 and then referred directly to outside agencies at Stage 3. Stage 2 of the Code is more appropriate for pupils at Key Stage 2 and beyond, where a 'continuing concern' persists despite the investment of additional class-based time and resources.

According to the Code of Practice, Stage 2 is 'triggered' by 'continuing concern' at a Stage 1 review or if discussions with parents suggest the need for 'early intensive action'. Among the survey schools, all of whom had previous experience of staged assessment, there was a sense that they had some idea what a Stage 2 pupil 'looked like'. Yet at the same time, there was a feeling that things would be 'easier' if they had 'guidelines' – or if they 'knew what other schools were doing'. In other words, they would be happy to agree some definitions and to work with other schools to achieve a consensus.

REFLECTION

- How clearly has your school or LEA defined the borderline between Stages 1 and 2?

FEEDBACK

Every teacher interviewed in the survey suggested that the most important distinguishing feature of mainstream pupils with special needs was reading difficulty. They agreed that most of the pupils on Stage 2 registers could be defined in terms of their reading difficulties. All the SENCos in the survey thought that at Stage 2 there should be a degree of objectivity about the 'trigger'. The best guarantee of that was the use of reading ages taken from standardized reading tests. The National Curriculum reading tests were seen to be neither as precise nor as reliable as traditional norm referenced tests (TES, 1995). The primary schools in the survey had all settled on a reading age two years below a pupil's chronological age as being a workable definition of Stage 2 learning difficulties. The secondary schools were happy to adopt the Warnock definition of two years and four months below.

The single most common 'trigger' to get a pupil across the threshold between Stages 1 and 2 was a reading difficulty. In other words: if the school had tried to support a pupil through extra time and suitably differentiated class work; and if the teachers were still worried and if the pupil still had a reading age that much behind – then he or she should be put on the Stage 2 register.

The survey schools agreed that the second largest group of pupils on Stage 2 registers had emotional and behavioural difficulties. Here it was much more difficult to achieve a consensus. The behavioural problems of 5-year-olds were seen as quite different from those of 16-year-olds. The problems of inner city pupils were reportedly more extreme than those in affluent suburbs.

One survey school included self-mutilation and demanding money with menaces in their list of 'typical' Stage 2 behaviours. Other schools had never had to deal with such serious problems. What linked these schools was that they all had clear disciplinary policies. These included precise rules for pupils which in many cases were posted clearly in every classroom. The staff had all agreed guidelines, which included advice about the kinds of support they could expect from colleagues, senior staff and outside agencies. The thresholds between the stages in the assessment procedures may have varied *between* schools, but they were consistent with the school's behavioural policy and appeared to be consistently applied *within* the school.

The use of staged assessment for behavioural difficulties was seen first and foremost as a means of monitoring and managing problematic behaviour in each school. The age of the children and the social context of the school had a bearing on what schools considered unacceptable. However, there was a degree of consensus within the group. Those interviewed agreed that before a pupil could be registered at Stage 2, there was generally a behavioural *pattern*. One single incident could lead to registration at Stage 2 or beyond if it was serious enough, but this was relatively rare. There also had to be *evidence* of problem behaviour, and the classroom teachers had to agree that the problem behaviours were no longer manageable within the classroom. There also appeared to be a level of agreement about the kinds of behaviour, which merited a Stage 2 individual education plan:

- persistent refusal to obey class teacher
- persistent refusal to work
- chronic disruption of lessons
- persistent bullying
- ongoing tantrums
- persistent truancy
- withdrawn behaviour.

As well as pupils with low reading ages, or emotional and behavioural difficulties, the survey schools also wanted to include six other groups of pupils on Stage 2 registers:

- low attainers, defined as pupils who were still working towards Level 1 at 8 or Level 2 at 11, despite extra classroom help and suitably differentiated classwork
- pupils with specific learning difficulties, defined in terms of a marked difference between cognitive ability and reading, spelling or maths
- more able and talented pupils, who would benefit from extra help and suitably differentiated work
- attendance difficulties, those pupils referred to Education Social Workers because their attendance fell below 80 per cent
- pupils with health problems which, according to their GP, the school doctor or school nurse, were affecting progress in school
- pupils with moderate sensory impairment, who were receiving school-based support from peripatetic services.

What emerged from the survey schools was that Stage 2 should be based on much closer definitions than those outlined in the Code. Not to tighten up would leave schools open to the criticisms made by the Audit Commission (DES, 1992) even before the Code was published:

> There is little consistency in identifying the children who need extra help. Further when extra help is being provided, it is not having the effect it should.

Wherever possible, the survey schools accepted that the Stage 2 criteria should contain educational measures, either in terms of norm referenced test scores or of National Curriculum levels or in terms of other agreed quantitative scores. These would underpin the way schools defined the pupils who needed additional help and the resources they needed to provide.

THE STAGE 2 IEP

If 60 per cent of the pupils in an urban school like Eastville would register at Stage 1 at some time in their careers, only 20 per cent were likely to be on the Stage 2 register. It is much more realistic to write an IEP (individual education plan) for the much smaller group of children referred, though even at this stage there is a case for making the form-filling as simple as possible, especially if large numbers of pupils are involved.

The IEP is not intended as a completely new approach. It is meant to include modifications to existing programmes of study, teaching strategies that are available within the school, special needs teaching and equipment that is available in the school, the more extended forms of pastoral care and disciplinary regime available for those whose behaviour cannot always be easily managed in class and medical requirements. It should also be built on close liaison between the child's teachers, the pupil and the parents (Butt and Scott, 1994).

REFLECTIONS

- What kinds of special provision are normally available in your school for pupils with:
  - reading difficulties
  - emotional or behavioural difficulties
  - learning difficulties
  - specific learning difficulties
  - physical or sensory disabilities?

FEEDBACK

For many schools already following a Warnock-style SEN assessment strategy, Stage 2 will be quite familiar. In all the survey schools, there are SEN teams which hold regular Stage 2 SEN assessment meetings. In the survey secondary schools, the whole team might include fourteen or fifteen people:

- the SENCo
- other staff with SEN responsibilities
- the pastoral management team
- the home/school liaison teacher
- the LEA behaviour support teacher
- the LEA learning support teacher
- the peripatetic teacher for the hearing impaired
- the peripatetic teacher for the visually impaired
- the school nurse
- the Education Social Worker.

The primary school teams were smaller (Harvey, 1995). Most teams met once a term, though there are often more regular meetings for sub-groups. At Eastville there are about six Stage 2 meetings a term for the SENCo, the pastoral team and the LEA behaviour support teacher. The main topics on the agenda are pupils who have already been discussed at the Stage 1 meetings, who are presenting continuing concern and who meet the criteria outlined in the Stage 2 descriptors of need.

The staff from the survey schools all had experience of staged assessment and they all felt confident about the kinds of special provision readily available to Stage 2 children in their schools. These included:

- withdrawal for reading recovery
- other small group support for the basic skills
- in-class support across the curriculum
- curricular modification and differentiation
- advice from teachers of the visually and hearing impaired
- advice from LEA teachers for specific learning difficulties
- advice from health and paramedical staff
- school-based counselling
- the disciplinary regime available in school for those whose behavioural difficulties cannot always be managed in class.

Some schools were even able to audit this special provision. In some of the survey primary schools, one afternoon a week had been set aside for the SENCo to see those pupils at Key Stage 2 with persistent reading difficulties. At one of the secondary schools all the pupils with a learning difficulty at Stage 2 could expect in-class support. At another secondary, Stage 2 pupils could expect a maximum of 10 per cent of curricular time for reading recovery withdrawal work – if their reading ages were two or more years behind their chronological age and they were failing to thrive with mainstream support. At Eastville, Stage 2 pupils with behavioural difficulties were seen for counselling or behavioural support at least once a week for six weeks by school staff.

Some schools were attempting to use two- or three-page proformas to record special educational plans for every Stage 2 pupil. These were taking the SENCo hours to fill in – and as a result the special provision was being *cut back* in order for the paperwork to be completed. Others had a more sanguine approach. They used a single top sheet for each pupil, with simple checklists, the main descriptors of need, the kinds of special provision readily available and short sections for:

- specific programmes/activities/materials/equipment
- curriculum modifications
- pupil and parent involvement
- agreed targets
- assessment arrangements
- review dates.

Additional detailed diagnostic information, for instance about reading or numeracy problems, or more detailed targets, for instance about managing specific behaviours, could simply be stapled on to the top sheet as required. This considerably reduced the time needed for paperwork and resulted in more individualized record keeping.

WHOLE-SCHOOL INSET FOR STAGE 2

It is clear that if there is to be a greater degree of consistency in school-based SEN provision, the borderline between Stages 1 and 2 is going to need much clearer definition. If these definitions are to be accepted by mainstream teachers, there needs to be at least an introductory programme of inservice training, which would ideally include:

- discussions with the outside agencies who monitor pupils at Stage 2
- discussions with parents and pupils
- opportunities to review the curricular modifications and differentiation normally available in the school.

In two of the survey schools, the SENCo and staff had access to all the programmes of study and differentiated support materials, but this was clearly unusual.

MANAGEMENT TASK

Design an inservice training programme for your school which would involve the whole staff in the production of a Stage 2 IEP.

- Single out a group of non-statemented pupils in your school who present continuing learning and behavioural difficulties and who raise issues of definition.
- Devise ways in which outside agencies could be of help.
- Devise ways in which parents and pupils could be of help.

FEEDBACK

In order to ensure that the whole staff understood the way that individual education plans worked, Westville – one of the survey schools – held an introductory two-day inservice training programme for all the staff. This began with an overview of staged assessment from the LEA SEN consultant, which clarified the main issues of the Code and showed how it fitted into whole-school assessment policies.

This was followed by a role-play exercise, where teachers played the parts of the parents of two pupils with learning difficulties who had just joined the school and a deputy headteacher who had been drafted in to prepare an IEP in the SENCo's absence. One of the 'parents' had literacy problems and a negative experience of school. The staff could talk to the 'parents' in role and advise the 'deputy' about how he could manage the situation. This led to a discussion about the role of the form teacher, the subject teacher, the head of department, the head of year and the senior management in SEN assessment.

The staff were then given an opportunity to meet members of outside agencies – the Educational Psychologist, the LEA learning and behavioural support teachers and the Education Social Worker – and to discuss their roles in school-based assessment. The following day there was a presentation by an LEA advisory teacher on the role of differentiation in Stage 2 IEPs. The rest of the morning was spent by staff meeting in departments with LEA advisory staff and producing differentiated materials and activities for a specific child in each year. This was written up as a departmental plan for these pupils:

- One had reading and attendance problems
- Two had learning and behavioural difficulties
- One was more able and had behavioural difficulties
- One had physical and learning difficulties.

On the second afternoon all the staff who taught that child came together with the psychologist or the learning or behavioural support teacher to pool their ideas and produce an individual education plan. One group included a pupil with special needs and her mother, who were both prepared to join the staff as co-trainers and participants. Though the training days had started with an outline of the procedures, the main emphasis of the rest of the programme had been on the children and the special provision that was normally available in the school. The aim had been to reinforce the concerns of the staff and reduce the anxieties that the very mention of IEPs seem to generate in some schools.

In some schools in the LEA, where the proportion of mainstream pupils with special needs is small, it is possible for SENCos to hold similar meetings about every pupil on the Stage 2 register twice a year and to involve all the subject staff in drawing up their own targets and writing their own individual education plans. Given that many of the problems associated with pupils at Stage 2 are relatively common, it could be argued that many such meetings may be redundant. In urban schools, where 10 per cent of pupils might be registered at Stage 2, or in inner city schools, where the figure can be twice or even three times higher, it is clearly impossible to organize comprehensive coverage, so it is essential to involve the whole staff in a training programme and establishing generic targets.

DISCUSSION OF STAGE 3

According to the Code of Practice, Stage 3 is triggered if external support is considered necessary, either because the individual education plan was proving to be ineffective or because of parental concerns. Stage 3 may involve referral to any one of a second tier of external agencies, including Educational Psychologists and those concerned with children's health. Referrals can seem quite an undertaking, but many schools already have a pre-planned cycle of meetings with outside agencies. Among the survey schools, Stage 3 meetings correspond to the enlarged Stage 2 SEN meetings. One survey school which held such a meeting during an OFSTED inspection was recommended for:

> a cycle of meetings with each area team. This provides the opportunity for the special needs of individual pupils to be discussed by year tutors with the SEN team and relevant representatives of support services. The meetings are well organized and recorded and information is promptly communicated to all concerned. The school makes good use of the help available from external agencies.
>
> (Eastville OFSTED report)

REFLECTION

• Does your school have a calendar of pre-planned SEN meetings for school-based assessment?

FEEDBACK

The SENCo of Southville Secondary School characterized pupils with learning difficulties on the Stage 3 register as those who 'have been withdrawn for extra help in reading, given in-class support, retested and still not managed to progress'. The SENCo would have been 'approached by staff to say they can't cope'. She would then have circulated the staff to see if this was the general view. The child's teachers would have asked her 'what more could they do?' The parents would have been seen and shown how to help the child at home, but they too would have accepted that 'the child has problems'. Only at this point would she have referred the pupil to an outside agency, like the LEA's learning support service or the Educational Psychologist.

The SENCo characterized pupils with behavioural difficulties on the Stage 3 register as those who have exhausted the whole range of Stage 2 monitoring and managing strategies, for whom there is 'a lot of evidence' of difficult or disruptive behaviour, or who have had to be removed from classes 'more than once a day'. There would have had to be 'frequent involvement of parents'. Suspected school phobia, eating difficulties, the involvement of psychiatrists or clinical psychologists or Social Services, the concern of GPs, school nurses, paramedics, LEA support staff or parents could also be sufficient cause for pupils to be registered at Stage 3.

A small number of children fail to thrive despite a Stage 2 IEP. For a pupil like Clara, who had a reading age of less than 7 and had failed to make any further progress despite additional reading help, targeted in-class support and a period of withdrawal to a special class, the Stage 3 meeting recommended a full investigation by the LEA learning support service, by the Educational Psychologist, by the school nurse and the Education Social Worker. The school was advised to try out a further range of special provision, curricular modifications or differentiations and to provide Clara with rather more time for small-group help. If no further progress resulted, her targets would be reviewed in six months.

THE ROLE OF EXTERNAL AGENCIES AT STAGE 3

In a small primary school in an affluent area, less than 1 per cent of the roll may be on the Stage 3 register. In an urban school like Eastville, this will probably involve 3 to 5 per cent of the roll in any one year; in inner city schools the figure could be twice or even three times as high. The IEP will include the advice of external specialists. LEA personnel, social workers or health trust agencies attending a Stage 3 Meeting do so as providers of support. Now that more and more of these agencies are working with schools on a purchaser/provider basis, the Stage 3 IEP may include a great deal more detail – with specific targets, and the frequency, duration and timing of interventions.

REFLECTIONS

- How much opportunity is there in your school for representatives from all the curricular and pastoral groups to discuss their continuing concerns with specialist teachers, medical specialists, Social Services or Educational Psychologists?
- Are the meetings with external agencies reactive, or are they written into your school calendar?

DISCUSSION OF SCHOOL-BASED ASSESSMENT IN STATEMENTING

For some children the statementing procedure starts before they reach school age, but for the great majority it comes about through a referral from a school. In some reception classes, pupils with extreme or marked difficulties are referred to outside agencies at Stage 3, without a delay for Stages 1 or 2. For older pupils, it is only after these first three stages have been fully addressed that statementing will be considered.

Six months after being placed on the Stage 3 register, Clara (see p. 37) was found to have moderate learning difficulties in reading. The psychologist discussed the possibility of initiating statementing with her mother. She suggested that this could lead to transfer to a special school, but both parents and school were happy for her to remain in mainstream class with the protection of a statement. This entitled her to rather more small-group support with basic skills, finely graduated tasks and in-class support for mainstream classes for as long as she needed them.

Stage 4 is the familiar multi-stage assessment, carried out by the school, health, educational psychologist and, if appropriate, Social Services. This may or may not result in the issuing of a statement. Stage 5 is the issuing of the statement. One of the new features of the Code of Practice is that while the request for a statement may be refused, the school may receive a 'note in lieu'. This means that while the LEA accepts that the child has special needs, the resources for special provision should be met from the school's existing resources. The Code includes a range of exemplars of the degree of learning difficulty which requires additional resourcing from the LEA within the protection of a statement and that for which the school should be liable from within its existing resources. The parents may challenge the issuing of a 'note in lieu' through a series of meetings with the school, the LEA and the new SEN tribunals (Rabinowicz and Friel, 1994).

Whether the child eventually receives the protection of a statement or of a 'note in lieu', the mainstream school will be asked for 'educational advice' at Stage 4. The content of Stage 4 advices varies between LEAs, but most ask the school to ascertain:

- the general health of the child
- cognitive ability
- communication skills
- attainments
- self-concept
- behaviour

- relationships.

The school is often asked to outline the special provision that it thinks the child needs. This includes an IEP. IEPs at Stages 4 and 5 may require an even greater level of detail than Stage 3 IEPs, such as:

- the subjects to be followed in the National Curriculum
- annual targets for these subjects
- long-term aims in respect of:

  - National Curriculum levels or GCSE results
  - work experience
  - FE provision
  - pre-vocational and vocational objectives

- levels of integration/small-group support
- teacher/pupil and SSA/pupil ratios
- support from external agencies
- targets for behavioural/medical/Social Services support.

CONSULTING PUPILS

Even for pupils with significant learning difficulties, the Code suggests that the wishes of the child should be taken into account. This builds on the good practice outlined in the Children Act. There should be regular conferences between form teachers and pupils from Stage 1 about the kinds of difficulties they may be experiencing and what the child can do to help. This is particularly important at times of transition – changes of school, option choice, work experience and YTS and college application (Wolfendale, 1992). With effective management procedures, the involvement of pupils in SEN assessment procedures can be planned into the round of whole-school guidance and counselling.

PUPIL PERSPECTIVES

For some pupils and ex-pupils, the processes by which special needs have been identified and assessed have been profoundly alienating, debilitating and destructive. They have been made to feel judged, humiliated and ignored. As one who had been assessed by three Educational Psychologists, one clinical psychologist, three social workers, three SENCos and innumerable Education Social Workers put it,

'What I dislike the most is when I'm in a meeting and they're talking over me. I feel like I'm a statue. People pick me up and move me around. I try to get a word in about me, about how I feel. But they don't listen. I want to lash out, just to stop them talking about me. It also makes me angry when people mess me around. They promise me something and then it breaks down. That happens again and again.

'It's better when they ask me to speak first. They'll ask me and I can have my say. They make me feel I can butt in and comment on what they're saying. The only times I come out of those meetings feeling good about myself are when I feel they've listened to me. I can tell them what I feel and I know at least there is someone who understands me. I can say what I feel and they come back to me and put my words in a different sort of way that helps me to understand my own situation better. Then I know that if I had a problem I could always go back to that person and they would understand me. Most of the time people say they understand, but they don't really.'

SUMMARY

The Code of Practice on the identification and assessment of special educational needs embodies a crucial shift in government thinking on SEN. It recapitulates Warnock's concern with the 20 per cent of pupils, nearly all of whom are in mainstream schools, who have some degree of special educational need at some time in their career. It consolidates the role of special education in mainstream assessment, and it infers that every classroom teacher is a teacher of special needs. It puts the 'expressions of concern' of classroom teachers at the heart of the first stage of the identification and assessment process, and it involves the pupils and their parents.

The 1994 Code also raises teacher concerns about increasing bureaucracy. Stage 1 registers can be kept very simple – with brief reference to *D*own to earth, *A*chievable, *R*ealistic and *T*ime-constrained action plans. They can be made the responsibility of every form and subject teacher. Individual education plans are reserved for Stage 2, but even these can be simplified. Most of the pupils on Stage 2 registers have relatively common and ephemeral difficulties, so their IEPs can be made easy to complete. It is only when pupils are exhausting a school's best efforts and external agencies are involved that more detailed SEN reports need to be made. An IEP at Stages 3 to 5 will probably be quite different from the Stage 2 variety.

In order to make the division of responsibilities between schools and LEAs equitable and consistent, it is essential to ensure that the borderline between Stages 2 and 3 is clearly defined by schools and that between Stages 3 and 4 is carefully monitored by LEAs. This has led schools and LEAs to develop moderating procedures. Some of these have already begun to generate lists of descriptors, prescriptions and guidelines. An example of one such 'Grid' is included in Appendix 2 (pp. 183–6).

The Code takes a gradualist approach to assessment reform, building on existing good practice in the Warnock Report and the Children Act rather then starting afresh. It also allows SEN Coordinators to manage change, involving the teachers who have the responsibility of raising standards of attainment in the first stages of identification and assessment. Appropriately managed reforms in identification and assessment procedures can be enhanced by school-based INSET, helping staff to develop a range of skills which will enable greater integration and the more effective teaching of pupils with special needs.

The views of the service users – that is to say, the pupils with special needs and their parents – can be neglected all too easily. Many felt that teachers did not know how to talk to them, how to let them take the lead in discussions about their needs, how to listen to them or how to reflect their views back to the meeting. The next chapter of this book will argue that this situation is unlikely to change unless teachers have more time and support to develop the appropriate skills.

The key role of listening emerged repeatedly during the research for both pupils and staff. During the turbulent period between the late 1980s and 1994, when the National Curriculum tests were being introduced and then constantly revised, the Special Needs Coordinators felt as if no one was listening to them. It was their 'concern' about the marginalization of pupils with low attainments, with emotional or behavioural difficulties or with the growing number of poor families that enabled so many of the survey schools to retain their sense of community, unity and direction. As a SENCo who was implementing the Code commented, 'It is essential that Coordinators make colleagues feel that they are being listened to'. The crucial place of 'expressions of concern' in the assessment process has pointed the way to a different, more inclusive educational philosophy.

3

Speaking and listening in the assessment process

INTRODUCTION

Speaking and listening to children with special educational needs is at the heart of the new identification and assessment procedures. As the Code of Practice makes clear, schools should listen to the views and wishes of pupils with special needs as part of the assessment process. Pupils with an IEP or a statement of special educational needs have 'important and relevant information and a right to be heard' (2.35).

It is somehow assumed that mainstream teachers can pick up this skill without special preparation (Cooper, 1993). There are teachers who lack the experience of talking and listening to pupils with special needs on an individual or small–group basis. They start their careers with only a partial understanding of these pupils' oral abilities or how to work with them to identify and assess their special needs (Powney and Watts, 1987). One of the recurrent criticisms of OFSTED reports is that pupils with special needs get too few opportunities to talk through their ideas with staff or their peers. Many teachers find it difficult to cope with the twin demands of maintaining good classroom discipline and managing informal discussions with individuals. Either they try to keep slow learners quiet, through forceful explanations, closed Yes/No questions, undemanding exercises and copying, or they allow pupils to chat aimlessly, thereby causing their lessons to lose pace and direction.

One way of bringing pupils with special needs into the assessment process and giving more serving teachers greater experience of informal talk with them is to offer a much wider range of mainstream staff inservice training in guidance and counselling for pupils with special needs. Most schools have records of achievement for all their pupils. The students with special needs can be divided among those with the counselling skills and experience. As more teachers become involved, the SENCo can begin to work with the Coordinators for Records of Achievement in English and pupil support as well as the staff concerned to coordinate speaking and listening objectives and to develop a more practical cross-curricular oracy policy.

OBJECTIVES

By the end of this chapter, you will have reviewed:

- Records of Achievement for pupils with special needs
- speaking and listening objectives for pupils with special needs
- your school's oracy policy for pupils with special needs
- the participation of pupils in drawing up an IEP or statement.

RECORDS OF ACHIEVEMENT

As long ago as 1973, David Lawrence found that counselling by non-specialists raised the self-confidence of slow learners and had a positive effect on their progress in reading. Most schools now accept the role of guidance and counselling in their pastoral work and preparation for records of achievement. In many schools, however, experience in counselling pupils with special needs is limited to a few 'expert' staff.

Records of Achievement were originally designed to provide those school leavers with few exam passes from areas of high deprivation with something positive they could show employers.

> We started off concerned about the fact that within our school there was a large amount being taught to the low achieving pupils in which they were doing quite well. They were obviously being motivated by it, they were obviously succeeding. We wanted to be able to give them at the end of their course something which was useful, we hoped, and something which recognised the amount of effort that they had put into it.
>
> (Sutton *et al.*, 1986)

They are now used across the ability and age range. Early research suggested that they may have had less effect on the employment chances of pupils with special needs than a range of exam passes, but that the opportunity for these pupils to discuss their own achievements with an interested adult is appreciated by both pupils with learning difficulties and their teachers. Schools which involve the whole staff in this kind of guidance and counselling have also noted an improvement in ethos and pupil oracy skills. And employers continue to rate speaking and listening skills highly, all other things being equal.

REFLECTIONS

- Which staff in your school help statemented pupils prepare their Records of Achievement?
- Which staff help those non-statemented pupils with special needs to prepare their Records of Achievement?
- What kinds of structures and safeguards are built into the process for staff with little experience of counselling?

FEEDBACK

At Eastville School, the opening of a 40-place unit for the integration of statemented pupils led the headteacher and a number of key staff to question the whole range of timetabling, staffing, assessment and special needs policies. In other schools this reappraisal of all the school policies associated with SEN assessment and provision has been seen as Stage Zero. It is not mentioned in the Code, but it seems a natural precursor to staged assessment. First, the Eastville group accepted that the most effective way of integrating statemented pupils would be to integrate the mainstream teaching staff. This implied that the staff all assumed a 'portfolio' of roles. Everyone would be invited to teach pupils with the full range of needs and abilities in small, safe, supported groups in order to learn how to prevent, assess and provide for the special needs of the pupils in their classrooms – now seen as Stage 1 assessment. Second, each would be given the opportunity to provide cooperative teaching in the mainstream, so as to be able to assess the needs of pupils who needed additional support at what is now known as Stage 2. Third, as many staff as possible had to feel comfortable about one-to-one guidance and counselling of pupils with special needs, so the topic was introduced to the staff as a whole through a two-day pro- gramme of training and workshops. Finally, a two-day training programme was organized about the place of speaking and listening in the National Curriculum for all children, including those with special needs.

The whole staff at Eastville had been involved in assisting all pupils, including those with special needs, to write their Records of Achievement for a number of years. There had been a programme of school based inservice training in guidance and counselling and a package of support materials for staff (DES, 1989). Most staff would see three or four Year 10 pupils and a similar number from Year 11 on an individual or small-group basis at least twice a term.

The match between student and mentor had to be carefully con- sidered from the start, but a widening group of mainstream staff had been enabled to get to know statemented pupils and non-statemented pupils with special needs. It is important that these mentors felt free to read the files and consult the qualified special needs staff, but in many instances they had been able to discover skills and positive attributes that were not in the official records, which did make a difference to career choices and helped to raise their self-esteem (O'Grady, 1993).

To take one example, Jodie was a statemented pupil with an unusual and complex genetic condition. This affected many of her internal organs, her hearing, her physical and sexual development and her learning abilities. It appeared that she had had a good start in the infants' class of her special school but that, because of her condition, her progress had then slowed and stopped. As her contemporaries approached puberty, her confidence ebbed away. She refused to wear the radio hearing aid prescribed for her and became isolated and depressed. Her emotional difficulties were compounded when her parents' marriage broke up. She did not even want to integrate into the mainstream classes, let along go on to college.

Jodie formed a very strong relationship with Mary, her mainstream Record of Achievement tutor. They gradually discussed some of the topics included in the tutors' guidelines:

- experience of school
- hobbies and out-of-school interests
- sporting activities
- tastes in music and clothes
- favourite television programmes
- plans when they leave school.

At first Jodie's speech was monosyllabic. She was unsure of what the teacher wanted from her and she was unused to talking about herself. Gradually she began to give more of herself and to speak at greater length. The tutor wanted to help, but at first it was very difficult. The breakthrough came when Jodie described a visit she had made to her GP. The doctor had obviously been concerned about her moods and had told her to visit his surgery whenever she wanted. One day she went to the surgery with Tim, a friend of hers from school who was a gifted draughtsman. The doctor had offered the two of them the chance to decorate one of the walls of his waiting room with cartoon animals. It was a large plain wall and Tim was enthusiastic. He drew the outlines and persuaded Jodie to help him with the painting. Then she drew some and painted them herself. Jodie had always thought she could not draw or paint. Now her work was being admired. Her father's new girlfriend was having a baby; so Jodie and Tim offered to paint a mural on the nursery wall.

Jodie's tutor's expressions of concern had elicited a long and well-organized narrative from Jodie. It also prompted Mary to raise the possibility of Jodie joining Tim's integrated art lesson. Later they negotiated Jodie's GCSE exam entry, as well as her admission to college to follow an integrated modular course for students with learning difficulties which included a mainstream art programme.

Until that time, of course, there had been no mention of Jodie's artistic talents on her official file. When the tutor and Jodie had begun to compile the Record of Achievement, the tutor approached one of the qualified special needs staff and said that according to the records, Jodie had moderate learning difficulties, and 'What should they put on the Record of Achievement?'

Getting pupils with special needs to reflect on their life stories in this informal way can often help us to see the person behind the disability. It can help to raise self-confidence on both sides and to develop the pupil's self-concept. The special needs teacher had been able to reassure Mary, the mentor, that the college was expecting Jodie to have learning difficulties, but that the work she had been able to help her produce in art was of a much higher quality than anyone had ever thought her capable of producing.

DISCUSSION OF THE ROLE OF THE DISABLED IDENTITY

The importance of labelling for people with disabilities and learning difficulties has been clear to researchers and practitioners for many years. American Social Interactionists like Howard Becker (1963), Lewis Dexter (1963) and John Holt (1964) realized that labels such as 'maladjusted' and 'backward' can lower teachers' expectations of pupils as well as students' own self-esteem. A late start in essential skills like reading can also make children feel 'dumb'. If something proves difficult to learn and is still beyond us after further effort and help, we are all apt to give up. Pupils learn to get by in class, without risking too much to themselves, by avoiding demanding questions. Staff respond by lowering their own expectations and limiting interaction to closed questions and requests.

John Holt believed that once pupils learn that they are 'failing', a teacher can only get the best out of them by watching them, listening to them and helping them to take risks again. British writers like Thomas (1985) and Lawrence (1991) have argued that:

> Enhancing the self concept of disabled children remains an important goal in education. It is not just a new system of educating disabled pupils by integrating them into ordinary mainstream classrooms [that is wanted], but a sensitive awareness of self perceptions. (p. 144)

One way of enabling staff to listen to pupil with special needs is for schools to involve a far wider range of mainstream staff in mentoring and counselling for individual and small groups of pupils with special needs. An alternative but complementary approach is through team teaching. This enables mainstream teachers to spend more time watching and listening to individuals and small groups of children with special needs rather than spending most of their energies on teaching and controlling the class as a whole.

REFLECTION

- In your school, is team teaching used proactively to enable a range of mainstream staff to observe and listen to SEN pupils?

FEEDBACK

At many of the survey schools, special provision for pupils at Stage 2 of the SEN assessment process involves a number of staff who are not in the Key SEN team. At Eastville, *ad hoc* groups join the special needs team for a year. During the Christmas term they help out with reading groups. Thereafter they work in their own departments, supporting statemented and non-statemented pupils with special needs. As part of the inservice programme, they are advised to spend two or three weeks observing these pupils to determine their special needs in National Curriculum terms.

By observing small groups in the mainstream classes, it is possible for some staff to realize that some of the students with apparent learning difficulties have a greater understanding than either the teacher or pupil previously realized, particularly if tasks can be presented in a different way. Bob, a 14-year-old, was at Level 2 in maths, a low achiever with little confidence in his abilities. Instead of working at a problem, he would whisper to his friends or copy their answers. His concentration was poor and if he could not see a solution straight away he would give up. He would chatter when the teacher was explaining the work and disrupt a class which was quietly working.

With a support teacher, who would get him to explain his ideas as he worked, he was able to stick with a problem much longer and show some insight. When the class was carrying out an investigation into the number of squares on a chessboard, Bob was not only the first to grasp the formula, he also predicted that it would hold good for a shape with nine square units – showing understanding at Level 5.

SPEAKING AND LISTENING ACROSS THE CURRICULUM

As the Dearing Review (1993) made clear, all the activities in all the subjects at Key Stages 1 and 2 will involve elements of the National Curriculum in English. Many aspects of the English curriculum are also thought to be 'relevant across the curriculum' at Key Stages 3 and 4. The Dearing Report reiterated the importance of oracy. The distinctive purpose of Key Stage 1 was to 'lay the foundations of future learning by developing basic skills' including 'speaking and listening'. It also emphasized 'the development and consolidation of the basic skills' including oracy 'through a range of subject content' at Key Stage 2. In effect, these strictures also extend to pupils of secondary age with special needs who are working towards Level 3.

The main objectives for speaking and listening in English for pupils at the lower levels of the National Curriculum are to develop 'confidence', incorporating 'relevant details' into 'explanations, descriptions and narratives' and choosing their words with 'precision'. They learn how to 'take turns' and to adjust their language to suit the listeners, the situation and the task. As they develop they begin to listen with greater 'thoughtfulness', to use questions 'that clarify their understanding' and to speak more coherently and take 'different views into account'.

The corresponding objectives for speaking and listening in maths included 'expressing themselves clearly', 'explaining their thinking to support the development of their reasoning', 'discussing their work' and asking questions. In science, they included 'expressing themselves clearly', 'communicating what happened during their work' and presenting 'scientific information in speech'. In technology, they included 'expressing themselves clearly' and using 'appropriate vocabulary'. Similar phrases recurred in all the other chapters of the 1994 curriculum orders.

REFLECTIONS

- What steps has your school taken to ensure greater consistency in the teaching of speaking and listening between subjects?
- How can you ensure that the progress of pupils in listening with greater concentration in some subjects extends to all?

- How can you ensure that pupils with special needs have the opportunity to speak at greater length in all subjects?

FEEDBACK

At Eastville School there were a few statemented pupils with severe learning difficulties. When they arrived at the school they were often very shy, especially in fully integrated classrooms. It was a major challenge to find topics and situations which allowed them to practise speaking clearly, responsively, with relevance and at length. Jane, for example, had cerebral palsy. She could walk with sticks, read the simplest of three- or four-letter words and count to ten. For most of her time at our school her father was terminally ill with cancer, and she would often burst into tears in the middle of lessons. Her speech was mildly dysarthric, extremely quiet and monosyllabic.

During a programme of study on the media, John, a mainstream English teacher, who was team teaching in Jane's classroom, started discussing television soaps with her. Suddenly, to his amazement, she started narrating the plots of *Brookside* going back over a number of years. She could remember details which everyone else in the class had forgotten. Because of her coordination and reading difficulties, Jane had never previously done any free writing. The team teacher started to write down some of these stories from dictation. Jane decided she would copy them up. Later, Jane contributed to her own Record of Achievement, and at college she learned how to write.

At about this time, Sally, the special needs creative arts teacher, was working on a new musical production. She felt that if she held Jane at the waist and helped her to talk her way through the sequence of steps, Jane could perform a dance solo. Through speaking and listening, team teaching, drama and role-play, pupils with a 'disabled identity' can learn to find new roles which offer more scope for their creativity and aspirations. It then becomes possible for them to use a mainstream audience to legitimate these raised expectations.

Salman was in the same class as Jane. English was his second language. He also had cerebral palsy and severe learning difficulties. Perhaps because of his difficulties in learning Arabic, gaining physical access to the mosque and taking part in fasts, he felt very insecure in his identity as a young Muslim. One day, he brought some photographs to school of his grandparents from Bangladesh. In the background, there was a mosque. Seeing the photographs, his RE teacher asked him to explain the main differences in Islamic family life between Bangladesh and Britain. This had the same liberating effect as Jane's lesson on television soaps. Salman began to speak at length and with concentration. He captured the interest of his class. He was the expert and they respected his authority.

Much of the work in enabling pupils with special needs to talk with greater confidence and authority in integrated classrooms depends on the accumulated efforts of teachers and peers rather than on these sudden isolated breakthroughs. In order to secure greater consistency in teaching styles, there needs to be an explicit, practicable and shared oracy policy.

THE ROLE OF AN ORACY POLICY IN PREVENTING SPECIAL NEEDS

Despite the strictures of the National Curriculum, it is all too common for teachers to assume that the act of speaking and listening is mainly the responsibility of English teachers or that the development of these skills in pupils with special needs should be left to special needs support teachers. Without careful curricular coordination, the pupils with special needs can experience considerable inconsistency, particularly 'where they spend one year with a teacher who encourages children to talk and another where it's mainly teacher's talk in the classroom' (Wilkinson, 1988).

One way of heightening staff awareness is through inservice training on oracy across the curriculum and ability range. It becomes easier to develop speaking and listening skills in pupils with special needs once a sizeable minority of staff have had the experience of working with individual pupils on a one-to-one or small-group basis through the production of Records of Achievement.

Some researchers and practitioners have posited a hypothetical 'Stage Zero' in the identification and assessment process. What they mean by this is that unless mainstream staff have effective whole-school assessment policies and programmes of study, certain pupils will develop learning difficulties quite needlessly. In other words, if schools have cross-curricular policies on the basic skills of oracy, reading, spelling, numeracy, and information technology, they could prevent some pupils' learning difficulties.

One of the SENCos from the survey schools argued that Stages Zero and 1 in oracy constituted the most problematic area in re-interpreting the Code for her school. It was relatively easy to decide which pupils needed special provision at Stages 1, 2 and 3 in reading and spelling, if only because there were easily applied group tests with norm referenced thresholds. Pupils with difficulties in maths and IT could similarly be screened out using written or practical National Curricular assessments. But the special needs of pupils who were quiet or inarticulate or who did not know how to respond appropriately to others' speech often escaped detection.

REFLECTIONS

- Have staff in your school had the opportunity to reflect on the NC document's advice on the role of oracy across the curriculum?
- Have staff made and shared examples of audio and videotapes of effective classroom talk in your school?
- Do staff share their perceptions of the place of talk in the classroom?
- Have staff discussed ways of improving the quality of classroom talk?
- Have staff discussed practical ways of observing, recording and reporting oral work?

FEEDBACK

Even where it is not possible to resource one-to-one support teaching for all the pupils with oracy problems in integrated classrooms, individual teachers with good classroom management skills can be encouraged to try strategies that will involve the less responsive, confident and articulate pupils. Some teachers have introduced pupil-led philosophical discussions (Lipman, 1980). Others have radically extended the role of pupil talk so that it begins to alter the character and form of the lesson (Dolan *et al.*, 1979). Instead of the traditional 'chalk and talk' approach, where the teacher explains the lesson, reads a brief passage from a textbook, asks questions to make sure the class was listening and then reinforces the points with a worksheet, the teacher can try a more 'interactive' approach. Here, pupils read part of the text and then question the teacher. The teacher still continues to dominate the tone and style of the lesson, but the pupils are enabled to negotiate the lesson content and direction.

When the teacher first starts this kind of interactive work, the pupils generally try to catch the teacher out. They ask questions about unimportant details rather than about the substance of the lesson. The teacher can reinforce effective questioning by scoring the questions, with higher marks for the more probing. Then, when the class has become used to setting the questions, the teacher can invite the class to answer each other's questions. Probing questions still get high marks, but so do effective and appropriate pupil answers. The very highest scores can be reserved for interactions between pupils which sustain discussions, raise original lines of enquiry or enable those who are shy or awkward or obtuse in ordinary lessons to sparkle. The teacher can even ask one of the class to act as score keeper. The criteria for grading talk can be made explicit, emphasizing:

- depth of questioning
- competence and precision in answering
- reasoning ability, the ability to infer or predict
- the ability to recall detail or marshal evidence
- the confidence to adjust their answers to their audience.

Interactive classrooms often encourage those pupils with little self-confidence or with divergent or original learning styles to take a leading role. Some pupils with special needs or special gifts may find this approach particularly exciting. They can begin to reflect on their own intellectual agenda and develop a clearer conception of their own learning needs.

Gary was a non-statemented Year 9 pupil of low average ability but with specific problems in writing. His special needs had been discussed at a Stage 2 meeting and it was clear that he tended to spend most of his energies avoiding written work in most arts and humanities subjects. As a result, he was still only working towards Level 3 at the end of Key Stage 3 in these subjects. When he did talk, what he said was often disruptive and irrelevant.

His English and French teachers were persuaded to set him more clearly defined oral tasks. Gary really took to interactive lessons on William Golding's novel *Lord of the Flies*. At first he asked questions to try and show up the teacher. This is a novel with a particularly transparent metaphorical structure, which often enables pupils with specific learning difficulties to make great progress. Gary was the first in the class to realize the importance of the imagery of pigs and pig hunting and to relate this to the character of Piggy. He predicted Piggy's death and its significance for the narrative structure. Having appreciated the author's techniques, he was then able to link Golding's descriptions of the island setting to his explorations of the character of Ralph – all Level 6 activities and much closer to his abilities in maths, science and technology.

There is a point in the novel when Jack decides to leave the main group and take his hunters with him. This is preceded by a lengthy description of the light on the two sides of the island. In answer to another pupil's question about the position of this descriptive passage in the structure of the novel, Gary confidently predicted Ralph's indecision and Jack's splitting of the group, an original insight probably more appropriate to Level 7.

Gary's enthusiasm had a tremendous effect on the class and it was then possible for the teacher to turn the discussion back to the point of reading, writing, talking and listening and how it was possible for pupils to take responsibility for their own individual educational plans across the curriculum.

PUPIL PARTICIPATION IN DRAWING UP AN IEP OR STATEMENT

The Code of Practice is quite clear about the involvement of the child in statutory assessment of special needs. Many LEAs have produced a pro forma especially for pupils. Even where pupils would have difficulties completing a form on their own without help from a teacher, parent or member of an outside agency, the Code suggests that the LEA may wish to have the views of the child set out separately from those of parents, teachers or agencies.

For non-statutory school-based assessment, the Code advises teachers to consult the child, even at Key Stage 1. In schools where all pupils have had the opportunity to discuss their own life stories or to reflect on their learning abilities and disabilities, this should present few challenges. It can be built into the school's normal procedures for involving the pupils in their own profiling and Records of Achievement and in the school's day-to-day counselling.

PUPIL PERSPECTIVE

At Eastville School, where the whole staff undertook a portfolio of roles including that of mentoring pupils with special needs, and where all the pupils, including mainstream pupils with no special needs, had a regular opportunity to discuss their progress with a personal tutor and set their own targets, there was considerable enthusiasm among the pupils for self-assessment. As Martin, a statemented pupil, explained,

> 'I would like to see my tutor more often. We only have appointments two or three times a term. Sometimes, the other kids have a go at me and I go and see my personal tutor, even if we don't have an appointment. It helps a lot, especially when you have to do your Record of Achievement. There's someone who knows you.'

Marie, another statemented pupil, recalled:

> 'I went to see my personal tutor a lot when they were organizing work experience. I wanted to work in a florist's, but it wasn't very easy to get a place. My tutor helped find me a place in a garden centre. That made it easier when we had to do my transition plan. She knew how well I did and she helped me get a good course at college.'

SUMMARY

Following the lead of the Children Act, the Code of Practice puts pupil consultation at the centre of the assessment process. For many schools, this is already part of the normal routine for SEN assessment, even for younger pupils and those with significant learning difficulties. Pupils routinely complete sections of their subject reports and profiles and write parts of their records of achievement. They also attend review meetings.

For a few schools, the involvement of pupils in self-assessment is the natural reflection of oracy policies which encourage task-related talk across the curriculum for pupils of all abilities, including those with special needs. Some would see the development of whole-school oracy policies as a necessary precursor to a special needs policy – Stage Zero in the identification and assessment process, which enables schools to prevent learning or behavioural difficulties occurring in some pupils.

In schools whose pupils have yet to be involved in the process, or where mainstream staff have little experience of individual or small group work with pupils with special needs, it may be helpful to start by involving small *ad hoc* groups of interested and sympathetic staff in helping pupils with SEN to produce their Records of Achievement. It is not unusual for these teachers to uncover unsuspected skills or other positive attributes. Staff can help pupils develop the self-confidence to enhance their transition plans and share the role of pupil advocate.

4

Inservice training in reading

INTRODUCTION

From the time that the role of Special Needs Coordinator was originally defined, responsibility for the development of staff expertise was seen as critical. This approach is maintained in the 'Code of Practice', which lists 'advising fellow teachers' and 'contributing to the inservice training of staff' as two of the main responsibilities of the SEN Coordinator (2.14). It also emphasizes that a school's SEN policy should describe plans for the 'inservice training and professional development of staff to help them work effectively with pupils with SEN'.

Working effectively with pupils with special educational needs can be one of the most demanding aspects of teaching. In many surveys, teachers cite this as one of the areas for which they felt least well prepared by their initial training. A few lectures and a little textbook knowledge at the start of a teaching career can also be dangerous things. Labels can be applied and expectations lowered. Many writers (e.g. Hannam *et al.*, 1984) argue that experiential approaches, based on informal teaching relationships in a safe situation, can provide a much more effective approach.

The Code does not specify the kind of topics that should be included in programmes of staff development or how they should be delivered. The main focus of the Code is on assessment – not on special provision nor the inservice needs of staff. However, every single teacher and headteacher interviewed as part of the moderation project thought that reading difficulties were the greatest issue for mainstream pupils with special needs. Recent studies, such as the ATL survey of teacher perceptions of National Curriculum reforms reported by Campbell and Neill (1994), confirm this picture. They suggest that staff are most worried about falling standards in reading. After all his consultations, Ron Dearing (1993) reported that 'The prime responsibility of teachers ... must be to ensure that all pupils make good progress in the basic skills':

The discussion in the consultation conferences confirmed the paramount need to provide adequate time for the teaching of basic oracy, literacy and numeracy. (4.17)

Harnessing these 'expressions of concern' about basic skills like literacy can provide Special Needs Coordinators with a starting point for whole-school SEN inservice training. This chapter will argue that in enabling mainstream staff to learn the skills of teaching and assessing basic literacy, SEN Coordinators can raise expectations and attainments. Even readers who have fallen well behind their peers can make rapid, short-term gains in reading when taught in small groups on a regular basis by non-specialist reading teachers. They also gain significantly more in the long term if the staff who have taught them to read also teach them their mainstream lessons.

OBJECTIVES

By the end of this chapter you will be able to:

- choose books for a small group of poor readers which they will enjoy reading and which are at an appropriate level for them
- assess their reading strategies
- develop a range of teaching strategies to improve their fluency, accuracy and comprehension.

DISCUSSION OF A COORDINATED STAFFING STRATEGY FOR THE TEACHING OF READING

In the years that followed the publication of the Warnock Report, there was a debate about the value of remedial reading. A number of writers argued that withdrawing pupils for extra reading help can damage pupil self-esteem and that it produces very little long-term progress (e.g. Simmons, 1986; Visser, 1986). There was a belief that children with special needs would feel stigmatized at being taken out of their regular classes and that they would gain more through in-class support. Partly as a result, far fewer SEN resources in either the primary or secondary sector are now devoted to withdrawal work on basic literacy.

Where small-group reading teaching does occur, it is often carried out by the Special Needs Coordinators themselves, SEN link staff or volunteer helpers. This often produces rapid short-term gains. The problem with this approach is that in many cases, pupils have returned to their mainstream class teachers, who may be using very different books and who may feel inadequate to follow up the work of the SEN specialist. As a result, the pupils fail to make continued progress. Their reading scores plateau, and there is very little long-term benefit. This effect, first noted by Collins in 1948, has tended to obscure the long-term benefits of a coordinated staffing strategy for the teaching of reading to poor readers.

There have been recurrent crises of confidence about falling standards in reading for the last hundred years (Newbolt Report, 1921; DES, 1975). What distinguishes the latest controversy (Lake, 1991; Francis and Turkington, 1992) is the focus on the lowest attainers in areas of increasing deprivation. The survey schools in Southville, one of the poorer urban areas, had carried out a longitudinal study of reading scores across their cluster in their first post-Code audit. They found that in reception class, 28 per cent had difficulty recognizing individual letters or words. In Year 2, 23 per cent were working at or below Level 1. By Year 6, 63 per cent were below the national average and by Year 9, 80 per cent.

The apparent endorsement by the government of Marie Clay's (1990) Reading Recovery approach has also rekindled the debate about the positive effects of small-group literacy teaching. Lingard (1994) argues that mainstream teachers can make a difference given 'no more than a moderate degree of inservice training and the reorganisation of existing resources'. Marie Clay has long advocated a staged approach to teaching reading, involving mainstream teachers with back-up from specially trained staff.

One inservice strategy which would enable more mainstream staff to feel more confident about the identification and assessment of learning difficulties is for the Coordinator to train interested colleagues in the teaching of reading and to get them to do much of the small-group work. This helps spread the expertise and involvement among a wider range of staff and across the curriculum, and it allows staff to build their assessment skills on their experience of special provision.

It is sensible, in management terms, to start with a small *ad hoc* group of enthusiastic and influential staff, so that they will carry others with them. The training in small-group reading tuition can be followed up with experientially based training courses in in-class support. This approach, known as 'Free Flow' (Sewell, 1988), combines tuition in the basic skills like literacy with the more conventional post-Warnock approaches. The author would argue that SENCos who involve a high proportion of staff in an array of different SEN strategies are more likely to enable children with a history of learning difficulties to make long-term progress.

In a coordinated staffing strategy for the teaching of reading, the SENCo selects a group of poor readers most likely to benefit from intensive reading practice. In the survey schools which adopted this approach, these pupils generally had a reading age two to three years below their chronological age. The inservice programme would help the *ad hoc* group of mainstream staff to:

- choose the most appropriate books
- assess poor readers' skills as they listen to them
- develop their teaching strategies.

Much of this is common sense. Most staff who volunteer for this kind of work have a faint recollection of how they learned to read. They also have a feel for the kinds of books that pupils want to read. With very little help, they can also learn how to analyse pupil errors and find their own ways of enabling pupils to overcome their difficulties. What they need is ready access to a range of attractive and appropriate books, time to develop these skills with small groups of pupils in a non-threatening situation and some friendly advice if they run into difficulties.

REFLECTIONS

- How many of the books are there in your school library which pupils with reading difficulties would enjoy?
- Would they like the look of these books?
- Do the books reflect what you know of these pupils' interests?
- Are they too young for them?
- Do these books reflect the way your pupils speak in terms of vocabulary and length of sentences?
- In fiction:

  – is the storyline exciting?
  – are the characters well defined?
  – is the dialogue realistic?

- In non-fiction, is the information clearly presented?

FEEDBACK

Having found books that a group of poor readers might enjoy, the reading coaches let them sift through the selection and pick out a few that they would like to read, then ask each of them to read aloud a short passage of about a hundred words. As a rough guide to the book's readability levels:

- three mistakes mean the pupil can read the book independently
- five mistakes mean that the pupil can probably understand the book
- ten or more mistakes mean that the pupil can only read the book with help.

There are more sophisticated approaches to the assessment of readability. The reading tutors can be shown how to administer a reading test and then use a simple readability guide, such as Fry's 'Graph' (1977), which is not copyrighted. The reading coaches may object that it is quicker for an 'expert' to choose the reading material. However, if the SEN Coordinator is aiming to raise general staff awareness about reading difficulties, he or she may feel that the process of involving pupils in choosing books and enabling colleagues to make their own assessments may produce other beneficial side-effects. It can help staff to choose departmental textbooks which are more appropriate to pupils' needs.

DISCUSSION OF THE FIRST READING LESSONS

What concerned many of the teachers in the Campbell and Neill (1994) survey was that since the National Curriculum had been introduced, teachers no longer had as much time to hear children reading. The power of listening is enormous. Well-inclined mainstream teachers with little or no experience in teaching reading will almost certainly find that, if they listen to pupils reading with sensitivity and their full attention, it is possible for them to build up a relationship of trust and acceptance which itself helps pupil concentration and confidence. For pupils who feel they are failing in school, small-group reading help can generate a 'feel good' factor, where the reading tutors constantly reassure and praise their pupils.

Poor readers appreciate all too well the primacy of reading in our culture. It is essential to be able to read with accuracy and fluency: illiteracy is often a bar to success in school, examinations and employment. As early as Year 2, primary children seem to know who is reading 'easy' books. Anxiety about reading failure is learned at the same time as the children take their first steps towards literacy. In the first two or three lessons when mainstream staff listen to their group, it can be helpful for them to be positive and reassuring, telling pupils words that they don't know, praising them for what they can read and talking to them about the book. There is little to be gained at this early stage in waiting for pupils to struggle to decode difficult or unfamiliar words.

REFLECTIONS

- What non-verbal cues can staff use to reassure the pupils that they are listening to them carefully?
- If a pupil hesitates on a long or unfamiliar word, how long should staff let him or her struggle before they help?
- If a pupil makes a mistake with a word but seems to grasp the gist of the passage, will you tell him or her what he or she has done?
- What should they do if the reader skips a line and becomes confused?
- What should they do if the reader makes a series of mistakes and becomes confused or lost?
- How should they reinforce the meaning of the passage?
- How can they reinforce accuracy and fluency?

FEEDBACK

This is a new way of teaching for many mainstream staff, and there are understandable anxieties about whether they are doing things the correct way. In fact there are few hard and fast rules, and the SEN Coordinator has to be prepared to listen to staff and reflect back to them what seems to be working best for them. There does however seem to be a pattern that develops as teachers and pupils get to know each other and become more confident.

The first few times that mainstream colleagues listen to poor readers, they often feel so anxious for them that they want to tell pupils all the difficult words or let members of the group tell each other. After the first few lessons, staff will pause a little longer for the pupil to work out an unfamiliar word by splitting it up or using the context. After further practice, they will also begin to feed back to the pupils just what kind of errors they are making. They will find ways of analysing clusters of sounds, of finding syllabic patterns and checking that what they read makes sense. As the tutors begin to win the trust of the readers, they learn to accept advice, not as criticism but as support.

DISCUSSION OF PARENTAL SUPPORT

According to the Code of Practice, an individual education plan should outline the help that parents can give at home. At Eastville School, the Special Needs Coordinator wrote to the parents, inviting them to a meeting where they would be introduced to their child's reading tutor and shown how they were being taught. They were assured that even six weeks' help with the reading homework programme would enable their children to make rapid progress.

Almost invariably, these meetings are extremely well attended (Barrett, 1987). Most parents are concerned to know what they can do to help, and grateful to the school for involving them. A simple demonstration of Topping's (1986) 'Pause, Prompt, Praise' approach is arranged. One teacher plays the part of a slow learner and another the reading support teacher. They stop and explain why the child makes the mistakes he does and how the teacher is trying to assist. An extrovert poor reader can generally be coaxed into giving a 'live' performance, as if he were reading to his parents at home. This can be followed up with a question and answer session with the panel of reading tutors on how parents can help. The parents can be offered a brief summary of the approach (e.g. Topping, 1986). Most will then want to talk to their child's reading tutor.

MISCUE ANALYSIS

Listening to pupils reading can be one of the most illuminating ways of finding out how they learn (Goodman, 1964). Each of us probably has our own ways of recognizing words and phrases, of decoding unfamiliar words, our own working hypotheses of what constitutes the reading process, our own ways of making sense of what we read and our own typical mistakes, hesitations and confusions. As one of the reading tutors at Eastville School pointed out, children who watch a lot of television no longer appear to read books in the same way that older generations used to. If you watch young children sitting next to a television screen and scanning it, then watch them scanning a page of print, you may find that the television influences the perceptions of print. The way today's pupils read is probably slightly different from the way children read in previous generations. Left to right sequencing will not seem as 'natural' as it used to.

A sympathetic concern with the way pupils read can be crucial for children who learn to read later than most of their peers. They carry with them all their memories of confusion and failure. What the majority of these pupils need most is a teacher who will try to win their trust and understand their reading strategies, strengths and weaknesses.

After the very positive, non-judgemental approach of the first reading lessons, staff can be encouraged to start gathering information in their mark books about the way their pupils read and reflecting on the patterns of errors and understandings. A difficulty can occur at any level of the reading process in terms of:

- word recognition
- knowledge of letter sounds
- word omission
- the insertion of incorrect words
- incorrect word association
- guessing a plausible alternative
- guessing on the basis of the first letter or syllable
- random guessing through a breakdown in understanding of the context
- exhaustion or loss of nerve.

On the other hand, colleagues may find that one of their pupils who makes a range of apparently simple errors can:

- read a sentence or two without help
- read some long technical words unaided
- answer comprehension questions about the book with little problem.

After nine or ten reading lessons, it might be helpful for the reading tutors to focus on one or more of the pupils in their group and try to analyse the patterns of success and error in greater detail. They may find it useful to make notes of the actual miscues on a prepared photocopy of a part of the text.

REFLECTIONS

- If a pupil reads any difficult words correctly, how can these be recorded?
- How can words that have been read incorrectly be noted?
- What code can be used for:

  – omissions
  – insertions
  – or punctuation errors?

- How can the pupils' own corrections be recorded?

FEEDBACK

These self-corrections can be particularly indicative, as they can reveal a great deal about the pupil's understanding of the context or his feel for the structure of the phrase or sentence. Pupils with reading difficulties may well have learned to guess unfamiliar words or phrases recklessly, either because they know the teacher will help them out or because they do not expect words on the page to make much sense; but those who can correct themselves are closer to becoming independent readers (Smith, 1986).

It may be helpful for the Coordinator to call a meeting of the reading tutors half-way through a term to discuss and begin to assess reading styles. These inservice sessions will come to life if they are run as an open-ended problem-solving group, with an audiotape of a poor reader together with an annotated transcript. A few extrovert pupils might even be persuaded to be videotaped as they read, in order to help the teachers learn how to help them. The fact that the staff know the pupil and the book they are reading gives this kind of INSET an immediacy and it also helps to lay the foundations for a shared view of special needs provision in a school.

DISCUSSION OF STRATEGIES FOR DEVELOPING PUPILS' READING SKILLS

Sensitive analysis of the way pupils read can help to provide clues for the development of each pupil's reading skills. An inservice meeting with the reading tutors can help in the sharing of expertise. A pupil who makes lots of phonic errors may benefit from a quick refresher course in letter sounds (Bryant, 1990). Many Coordinators will have packs of such exercises readily available (Hornsby *et al.*, 1975). A pupil who can read long words but who makes persistent errors in simple word recognition may need to focus on accuracy. The tutors will have their own ideas about setting up a friendly competition. One tutor at Eastville School marked off a hundred words of the text and then challenged all his pupils to score as close to 100 per cent as they could. The score would be noted down and the next time he or she would have to beat the previous best score.

Pupils who read with little or no awareness of punctuation or who read without inflection may need some help with this. Another reading tutor at Eastville School got his group to clap once for a comma, twice for a full stop and three times for a paragraph. There was often laughter and confusion while pupils learned to *see* the punctuation, but the pay-off for the pupils' written work was quite noticeable. Pupils who read one word at a time may be helped by quick 'cueing' sessions. Another reading tutor would read a passage to the reading group from their own book, leaving out key words, which the pupils would have to guess. Pupils with good phonic skills who seem to have limited comprehension might be helped if the teacher stops them at the end of a page and asks them to try and guess what happens next. Pupils who are easily discouraged or who make so many mistakes they sometimes lose the thread of a passage may need considerably more support with this. Another tutor would often ask each of the pupils a comprehension question at the end of the page, so that the pupils who were lost could recollect the narrative.

This may sound complex and difficult, but most pupils with mild learning difficulties make rapid progress so long as teachers are well inclined towards them and use their common sense. Most teachers also pick out their own preferred strategies. In the twenty years that the author has been keeping records of the progress made by poor readers in groups led by mainstream subject staff, the average gain has rarely fallen below 15 months in reading age during a one-term intensive reading programme. Some mainstream staff have managed average gains of 22 months in a three-month period. Exceptional pupils manage three or even four years' progress, though a very small group with more complex needs may actually regress. Lingard (1994) found very similar progress in those pupils taught to read by mainstream staff. He suggests that this rate of progress can be four times greater than that of pupils who merely received conventional 'post Warnock support'. Retested at the end of the year, the progress of these pupils does slow, but as long as there is a sizeable group of mainstream teachers providing both the reading tuition and follow-up in-class support in their mainstream lessons, they maintain most of their progress in the long term.

In schools where a poor reading age entitles pupils to extra reading tuition at Stage 2 of the identification and assessment process, the Coordinator can feel confident about passing on diagnostic information about reading problems to classroom teachers in the Stage 2 IEP. In schools where very few staff have actually taught pupils to read, however, data about pupils' weaknesses in phonics, fluency or comprehension might mean very little. Schools like Eastville, which have employed a rolling programme of inservice training and see all staff as Basic Skills Teachers, might welcome a reading profile on every pupil with a history of reading difficulties.

REFLECTIONS

- How much information is given on your school's IEP about reading difficulties?
- How many staff understand diagnostic information on reading difficulties?

FEEDBACK

There are a very few pupils who need considerably more experienced support than a Free Flow teacher can give. In certain areas of high deprivation some researchers have found an increasing number of Year 6 pupils without even the skills of basic word recognition or phonics (Lake, 1991; Francis and Turkington, 1992). Most of these pupils can achieve rapid progress using skills training programmes like DISTAR. This programme is based on direct instruction and reinforcement of phonics. It was first employed as part of the 'Head Start' initiative in the most deprived parts of the USA and was by far the most successful approach used there (Becker, 1977). It requires special training and, as the skills have to be kept in fairly constant use, it is sensible to confine this approach to specialist SEN staff.

By employing mainstream staff, who have been trained on site in the teaching of reading, to teach the majority of poor readers, together with specialized SEN staff for pupils who have barely started to read, it is possible to teach all but a hard core of 1 to 2 per cent of children to read. The broad mass of poor readers require a Stage 2 individual education plan, indicating that they have reading difficulties and that they need either intensive practice or initial reading help. Additional diagnostic information can be provided on the Stage 2 IEP, so long as there is a sizeable number of staff who can use it. As the Code of Practice indicates, pupils who fail to progress, despite regular reading practice or a special programme like DISTAR, will probably need the support of an external agency – the LEA learning support service or an educational psychologist and a Stage 3 IEP. Some of the survey schools quantified this. Pupils whose reading age had advanced more slowly than their chronological age despite small-group literacy support were given a Stage 3 IEP.

There will be children in most schools who make very limited progress in reading, despite intensive school-based help. It will not always be possible for the Coordinator to distinguish these pupils from the broad mass of poor readers in advance. Luckily, they are extremely rare. These pupils will be referred on to assessment at Stage 3, requiring additional input from outside agencies. Because they meet pupils with more complex or unusual difficulties, agencies like learning support or educational psychology may be able to suggest or provide approaches that the school cannot. There are many specialist phonic programmes, computer programmes and teaching strategies that are designed to overcome problems of visual or auditory perception available for pupils with these kinds of specific reading difficulty. Occasionally, the children's difficulties are so idiosyncratic that a completely original approach has to be developed.

Charles had a history of autistic-type behaviour. He tended to read very slowly, decoding each letter phonetically and only then reading out the whole word. He could spell out a word on one line, see the same word three lines later and fail to recognize it. As a result his word recognition score was like that of a typical 8-year-old. According to his statement, he had idiosyncratic perceptuo-motor difficulties and semantic/pragmatic linguistic difficulties. He had problems in recognizing shapes and in understanding that words on a page related to words used in conversation. Charles had a vivid imagination, a wide vocabulary and a strong grasp of metaphor. As a result, his reading comprehension was at Level 7 in the National Curriculum. He needed the protection of a statement, which ensured that he always had an adult to assist him with decoding on a one-to-one basis.

MANAGEMENT TASK

It could be argued that unless staff have had the experience of teaching pupils to read, they will not be able to utilize diagnostic information about reading difficulties or make much use of it in their classroom teaching. It is the SENCo and the other SEN staff who retain ownership of the IEP. If a sufficiently large minority of staff have undertaken the reading programme, the Coordinator could ask a group to design a reading profile for the Stage 2 IEP (see Appendix 1, p. 181). Mainstream staff would then take responsibility for it. The profile could include such data as:

- the pupil's reading age before SEN provision started
- the accuracy rate per hundred words once during every reading lesson
- a list of actual miscues,

as well as brief references to the concerns outlined in the National Curriculum English document like:

- notes on the pupil's fluency, style, inflection and use of punctuation
- comments on understanding of character, setting, storyline
- comments on the pupil's abilities to form inferences and deduction,

and notes of guidance from the reading teacher to mainstream staff like:

- strategies used by the reading teacher to promote accuracy, fluency, inference and deduction
- ways used to help reinforce understanding of narrative structure

- ways used to focus attention on character, setting, humour
- strategies to motivate the pupil to develop his or her own research
- ways used to help the pupil differentiate between fact and opinion.

PUPIL PERSPECTIVE

Many pupils are puzzled when told they have a low score in the basic skills, because, by their own lights, they already have some competency. However, they often sense that there is something amiss. They may avoid reading aloud in class; or they may develop compensatory classroom survival techniques (Holt, 1964). As one pupil put it, 'I didn't realize I had a reading problem until I came to reading classes'. There is little doubt that for many of those with poor reading, there is a stigma attached to joining a small group for special provision, as the critics of remedial reading pointed out. Initially, some pupils – like Leigh Anne – try to keep it from their parents. 'I didn't tell my mum I had reading lessons till a few weeks later. I didn't want her to know and I didn't want her to help!'

Especially sensitive tutoring can be a way of ameliorating this stigma. Tactful management of the first few lessons can be appreciated many years later, as another ex-pupil recalls. 'When I went to reading, I was introduced to everyone. I had to read a few lines out loud at first but it was all right and I made friends in the group.'

In retrospect, some ex-pupils were angry at the way earlier teachers had not grasped the nettle and given them small-group help as soon as they had begun to fall behind. Having undertaken a reading programme, been retested and told they had 'passed' provided some young adults with reassurance years afterwards. 'I had a test and I passed. I felt good. I still don't like reading aloud and try to get out of it if I can. But I know I can do it.'

Another ex-pupil commented 'I am glad I had the reading help. At first I was embarrassed, but it was OK later. I couldn't have managed without it.'

SUMMARY

The Code of Practice has undoubtedly given mainstream special education much needed confidence. Although the Code refers to special provision and inservice training, its main focus is on identification and assessment. This is very fully detailed, while SEN provision and its possible effect on mainstream teachers is more lightly outlined. As a result, the cyclical nature of assessment is neglected. Teachers understand more fully about special needs after they have tried to do something about them. The experience of providing special needs support helps staff understand special needs assessment.

There is an undeniable concern about basic literacy in the country at large among mainstream and SEN staff and parents. It was the single most important issue in mainstream special needs provision for every single teacher and head interviewed in our survey. This concern could be harnessed in an experientially based inservice programme to enable a wide range of mainstream staff to teach a basic skill like reading. This can provide a starting point for the raising of staff awareness of special needs and how they can be assessed. INSET can start with an *ad hoc* group of enthusiastic and influential staff, and then gradually involve a larger group as the demands of the school timetable permit. In this model, learning how to assess reading difficulties *follows* the experience of teaching reading.

It may need to be stressed that the first time a non-specialist hears poor readers read, both they and their pupils might need a great deal of reassurance and praise. For most children, including those with special needs, the teaching of reading is based on common sense. However, a slow start in reading is something that has huge significance in our society. It can affect pupils' self-esteem and self-confidence. Parents can be brought in and their help can make a positive difference, though this needs to be handled with sensitivity. With a combined approach from school and home, pupils can make rapid gains. This in turn affects their self-confidence across the curriculum and for years afterwards.

Miscue analysis can provide a start for the assessment of reading difficulties at Stage 2 – as well as their remediation. There are no hard and fast ways of teaching reading to pupils who have a history of learning difficulties. Keeping a reading log can help colleagues to analyse a pupil's reading style, strengths and weaknesses and to reflect on their own teaching strategies. The reading log can enable staff to work out ways of helping particular children and provide insights into the complexity of the reading process. This in turn often stimulates staff interest in learning about how pupils with special needs use their language structures in speaking, listening and writing.

Once a sufficiently large minority of staff have been involved in the teaching of reading, this begins to affect what writers like Gary Thomas and Anthony Feiler (1988) refer to as the 'ecology' of learning in a school. Greater staff sensitivity to the range of reading abilities in a classroom can enable poor readers to make better long-term progress. Staff who are more aware of the nature of pupils' problems often plan their purchase of textbooks more carefully and they are more likely to differentiate their use of materials and activities. They are also more likely to understand diagnostic data on Stage 2 individual education plans and respond appropriately.

Most pupils make rapid progress on an intensive reading practice programme, particularly if it is followed up with in-class support. The two approaches are not contradictory as is sometimes supposed, and they can both make an important contribution to school-based SEN inservice training.

The few pupils who lack even basic literacy skills often respond to regular direct instruction, including phonics teaching. However, there is a tiny minority who, despite intensive help, make no significant progress and fall further and further behind their peers. These pupils should be referred to Stage 3 of the identification and assessment procedure, allowing the school to consult external specialists, like the Educational Psychologists, who would then cooperate in the writing of an IEP.

Some of this tiny minority of pupils may have specific learning difficulties, which is to say that they have significant difficulties in that area which are not typical of their general or oral ability. Some may have reading difficulties as a result of particular emotional problems. Some may have perceptual difficulties related to a medical condition. Some may have moderate learning difficulties. A very few may find it difficult to learn to read for reasons that even the most experienced SENCos do not fully understand. Some of this tiny minority who do not respond to a Stage 3 IEP for specific learning difficulties in reading may require the protection of a statement and the additional resourcing that goes with it.

—5——————————————

Differentiation

INTRODUCTION

The Code of Practice suggests that when a teacher, parent or member of the outside agencies declares an 'expression of concern', it becomes the responsibility of form and class teachers to consult the Special Needs Coordinator and 'explore ways in which increased differentiation of classroom work might better meet the needs of the individual child'. Special help at Stage 1 may involve 'a period of special attention or carefully differentiated teaching within normal classroom work'.

The main focus of the Code is on assessment rather than special provision or inservice training. There is little doubt that class or subject teachers will need further training in order to provide special materials or activities, or that SEN Coordinators will be able to organize and manage the special attention without further inservice work. While a few LEAs have employed consultants to train SENCos and mainstream staff, many schools are having to improvise. What this chapter aims to provide is a school-based inservice approach, whereby class and subject teachers and Special Needs Coordinators can work together to produce differentiated strategies which reach out more effectively to pupils with special needs in mainstream lessons. It also seeks to examine ways of reducing the need for labelling and segregation and the unnecessary paperwork.

OBJECTIVES

By the end of this chapter, you will have reviewed:

- school-based INSET on differentiation and in-class support
- the problem of labelling and the context of differentiation;

and produced teaching plans for:

- differentiated teaching styles, resources and activities across the curriculum
- pupil groupings and individualized learning.

REVIEW OF A COORDINATED STAFFING AND INSERVICE TRAINING STRATEGY

In Chapters 3 and 4, we looked at ways in which the Special Needs Coordinator could harness the concerns of mainstream class and subject teachers to generate school-based inservice training on oracy and literacy for pupils with learning difficulties. Small groups of mainstream staff could be co-opted into special educational provision for short periods in order to learn how to develop pupils' speaking and listening skills through the creation of a record of achievement or how to teach them to read. This 'free flow' of expertise between the SENCo and the rest of the staff simultaneously raises awareness of the special needs that these children may have in 'normal classroom work' and provides special attention in basic skills (Sewell, 1988). Carefully managed INSET programmes can gradually ensure that a majority of the staff undergo this kind of consciousness raising and skill development and thus begin to change what Thomas and Feiler (1988) call the 'ecology of the school'.

Some of the 'free flow' staff involved in reading or oracy support spontaneously set to work, revising teaching materials and extending classroom activities in order to involve pupils with learning difficulties more successfully. Having joined a reading recovery group, one teacher was so horrified to realize the implications of her work with slow learners that she immediately threw out her old stock of history worksheets and produced a range of new materials. Working on her own, without any help from the rest of the department or the LEA learning support service, she designed differentiated worksheets for pupils of average ability, extension materials for the more able, support materials for the poor readers, a new drama-based approach to her work on the Spanish Armada and a film project. Most mainstream teachers appreciate extra time and inservice training in order to rethink their approaches, however (Peter, 1992). It is clear that the government has no plans to fund inservice training on differentiation nationally. As Mittler (1992) argued:

> The difficulties experienced by schools and services in part reflect the low priority and hence the low level of resourcing. This in turn is reflected in limited training and opportunities for continuing professional development. Such courses as have been made available tend to be short, sharp and school-based.

The rest of this chapter is based on the assumption that if a school wants all areas of the curriculum to be adequately supported, it has to develop its own coordinated special provision and INSET strategy.

Mainstream teachers who have been released from class teaching for a few lessons each week in order to take part in one-term oracy or literacy basic skills support programmes can then be re-timetabled for in-class support and the development of new differentiated materials. Instead of carrying out all the support himself or herself, the Special Needs Coordinator can begin to delegate. Given the complexities and very specific demands of the National Curriculum, it is far more effective for history specialists to provide cooperative teaching within their own departments, science specialists to support in science, and linguists in French or German – and then to base their differentiated materials on firsthand experience.

Change begins to ripple through a school. The SENCo can now call on a widening pool of staff across the curriculum, who are confident in their own subjects as well as being more sensitive to pupils' special needs. Subject specialists – who are aware of the National Curriculum level descriptors for pupils at the extremes of the ability range in their own subjects – themselves act as agents of change. No longer will the SEN support teacher have to act as a generalist, reading up the subject as he or she teaches it and trying to keep more than a lesson ahead of the pupils.

A Coordinated SEN staffing approach can also provide headteachers with a relatively painless way of redirecting resources into special needs provision. Given the pressures on governing bodies from Circular 6/94 to balance the amount devolved from LEAs for SEN in their LMS budgets with the amount they are actually spending on SEN provision, heads are reviewing their staffing options. Instead of taking on new full-time special needs specialists, some of the lessons of existing subject specialists can be given over to producing differentiated materials, withdrawing pupils for short periods of extra skills training and providing in-class support within their own departments. The SENCo can be contracted to work more closely with those departments for that year and either provide inservice training in the ways outlined below or organize others to do it. And the whole SEN package can be audited in terms of raised reading and maths scores and better SATs and GCSE grades for the target groups.

REFLECTIONS

- How much time is available in your school for mainstream staff to prepare a range of differentiated materials and activities?
- How does your Special Needs Coordinator enable staff to develop their range of resources?

FEEDBACK

Marion Clarke, a teacher at Eastville School, had a daughter with mild learning difficulties and when the opportunity came to join the SEN support group she was very enthusiastic. First she taught mainstream slow learners to read. Then she took over a small group of statemented pupils with physical disabilities and moderate learning difficulties for her own subject – geography. She started to create a new range of resources, activities and assessments, which would enable these children to follow the Key Stage 3 syllabus at Levels 2 and 3. It did not take long for her to realize how valuable these would be in her mainstream lessons and she began to use them with non-statemented pupils who had mild or specific learning difficulties.

Later, when the school brought in an LEA learning support teacher to develop its inservice training in differentiation, Marion volunteered to work with her. The LEA teacher had access to a wider range of materials developed in geography by other schools and authorities and a wider view of differentiation. Marion was time-tabled to work with her for a term, developing differentiated materials and activities, while providing cooperative teaching in her own department. She was given a brief to support statemented pupils in integrated lessons and to disseminate the new differentiated materials and activities in her own department. If one of her colleagues wanted to raise any concerns about a pupil with learning difficulties, it was to Marion that they looked, rather than the SENCo.

DISCUSSION OF LABELLING AND THE CONTEXT OF DIFFERENTIATION

Differentiation can be handled insensitively, and produce unforeseen and negative consequences. It was one of the defining concepts of the National Curriculum. Together with 'access', 'entitlement' and 'delivery', it supposedly guaranteed pupils with special needs a broader education, a wider range of subjects and a greater variety of teaching methods. In one of the earliest and most authoritative statements on the National Curriculum, Deidre Fordham of the Special Education Division of the DES argued:

> All pupils share the same statutory entitlement to a broad and balanced curriculum framework and specific provisions in it will offer very wide scope for teachers to deal with the full range of individual needs.
>
> (Fordham, 1989)

These central notions have not been without their critics, however. Some writers (e.g. Ball *et al.*, 1994) have argued that they offer a rationale for the transfer of educational resources away from the most vulnerable to high status groups. These are complex arguments which relate to a wider governmental agenda, but they have an important bearing on the way differentiation can be introduced.

One of the issues that provoked unease was the way these key ideas related to the other concepts underpinning government reforms, like 'choice' and 'diversity'. The House of Commons Select Committee has raised the possibility that a wider choice of local schools has led to greater social differentiation, if not 'polarization'. Schools in areas of greater deprivation have been losing pupil numbers to those in more affluent areas – and therefore income. There is a very high statistical correlation between levels of deprivation and numbers of pupils with special needs. Indeed, most LEAs still use the proportion of pupils on the free school meals register as a way of allocating mainstream SEN funding. If greater parental choice actually meant that schools in more affluent areas were using their power to select pupils who were of average or high ability and to 'deselect' those who needed more expensive school-based support at Stages 2 and 3 of the Code, it could be argued that one of the consequences of greater 'choice' and 'diversity' could be an impoverishment of opportunities for pupils with special needs in the most deprived areas. Just how this can work is made clear in Vincent *et al.*'s (1995) study of 'Waldergrave School':

> 'We're seen as a school of low achievers, there's no doubt about that.'
>
> (Chair of Governors)

> 'We would very much like a wider range of ability from several of our intake schools. We don't [get that]. What we do get is one or two who are directed to us, because we're good at special needs.'
>
> (Headteacher)

The ambivalence of the term 'entitlement' has been criticized in very similar terms. It may not always guarantee an improved service for the more deprived members of the community, as it seems to imply. This has been argued most forcibly in relation to government health reforms. National Health Service dentists, for instance, had found that they were no longer able to provide as full a range of services free to all at the point of delivery. In 1992, patients' 'entitlements' were limited to 'treatment necessary to maintain your oral health' (Form FP: 17: DC/GP: 17: DC). Other treatments – deemed to be 'mainly cosmetic' – had now become unavailable under the NHS, and patients were advised that they 'may choose to have these privately'.

In other words, for the NHS, 'entitlement' meant a more restricted general service, which was to be clearly distinguished from the privileged treatments reserved for those with the money for 'choice'.

The small print of the 'entitlements' needs to be read. Staff in the survey schools often pointed out that mainstream pupils with special needs have an 'entitlement' to a modern foreign language, but not to small-group reading help.

Some writers, like Len Barton (1986), have expressed the fear that the pressure to differentiate the curriculum could lead to more labelling, increased streaming and the segregation of pupils with special needs. There could be greater polarization between the extremes of the ability range, lowered expectations for the less able and an impoverished education for those with special needs. So far, there is little evidence about the effects of the National Curriculum on less able pupils – except the Audit Commission's critique (DfE, 1993), which concluded that pupils with 'particular needs' in urban schools appear not to have benefited from its introduction.

It is arguable that differentiation must be introduced with care. It may enable some pupils in some schools to play a fuller part in integrated classrooms and to achieve greater progress, especially if:

- it fosters an ethos of trust and mutual respect
- it enables pupils to raise their expectations, gives them an experience of success and raises their self-esteem
- it provides pupils with tasks that are matched to their abilities, interests and experience
- it allows pupils extra teacher time and support with unfamiliar or difficult tasks.

However, it may also work against the development of a more inclusive class or school ethos, especially if:

- the differentiated materials are ill-matched to the pupils' abilities
- they are insufficiently interesting or challenging
- they are presented in such a way that makes the users feel uncomfortable, powerless or stigmatized.

The content of the materials and activities and the context in which they are presented can help staff to reach out more forcefully to pupils with special needs – or reinforce lowered expectations. These are some of the general issues with which some SENCos have introduced their school-based inservice programmes on differentiation.

REFLECTIONS

- Do staff in your school plan their 'chalk and talk' lessons so that they use a mixture of unfamiliar and familiar words, simple and unusual illustrations, straightforward and more demanding questions?

- How do staff handle mistakes and wrong answers?
- Are the readability levels of the support materials in your school ever checked against the pupils' reading ages?
- Are the conceptual levels checked against the pupils' abilities?
- Are the tasks checked against the relevant National Curriculum level descriptors?
- How wide is the range of activities offered?
- How wide is the range of ways pupils can record their work?
- How much choice is built into the provision of differentiated materials?

FEEDBACK

Pupils are very quick to pick up that one group is being offered 'easy work'. Members of the special group may be called 'stupid' by their classmates and feel they have little incentive to improve. Sarah was a Year 7 pupil with a long history of intervention from LEA learning and behavioural support services and from Social Services. She enjoyed the extra attention and the easy work. On transfer to secondary school, this led her to pretend that she could barely read, when in fact she had a reading age of 9. Differentiated work was created for her at a level that was well beneath her capabilities and she spent most of her lessons dreaming, rarely completing the tasks she had been set. When her reading was retested, the SENCo spoke to her mother and realized the problem. She was then given work that was better matched to her abilities and she began to thrive.

DISCUSSION OF DIFFERENTIATION BY OUTCOME

One of the commonest teaching strategies is differentiation by outcome. The class is given the same activity to carry out or the same extract to read. The pupils may be set the same task to carry out, but would be expected to work at their own pace or produce solutions that were suited to their aptitudes. Or they might read the same piece, but be given a series of graduated questions to answer. The first few may be relatively easy, the next more demanding and the final set really extending. The class would be expected to answer as many as they were able. If the slow learners only managed to complete the first few, they would be allowed to feel that they had done a good lesson's work.

Common though this approach may be, it is one of the most difficult to manage effectively. Pupils who work quickly may rush through all the work, only partially understanding the more demanding aspects of the tasks. Slow workers may feel understimulated and can easily become discouraged.

TEACHING ASSIGNMENT 1

For one of the lessons you are planning to teach in the next week, design a piece of work that is differentiated by outcome. Try to ensure that:

- the tasks or questions you have designed for pupils with learning difficulties are in fact manageable
- these tasks are as interesting as the more demanding ones
- they include the full range of attainment targets appropriate for their level in the National Curriculum.

FEEDBACK

The head of modern languages at Eastville School had volunteered to join the SEN support group for three lessons a week for one year. He spent the first term working with a group of poor readers. His results were exceptional. Two of the group had more than three years' progress in that term. For the next term, he switched to providing in-class support in Year 8 French lessons and developing differentiated materials and activities for them. He invited the LEA advisory teacher into school to meet the department. They started their INSET programme by discussing a typical oral exercise – ordering in a café. It was decided that during the 'chalk and talk', the teacher should randomly mix familiar and unfamiliar, closed and open questions. From some pupils a simple *oui* or *non* was sufficient. Others were expected to repeat an appropriate noun from a list. Others would be expected to use the correct form of *de* or *du*. The most able would be encouraged to produce full sentences.

DISCUSSION OF THE SIMPLIFIED WORKSHEET

The second most common kind of differentiation is the simplified worksheet. There may be a departmental policy to use a particular textbook, as it covers the syllabus well. However, the textbook's readability level can put it beyond the reach of pupils with reading difficulties and the tasks may require comprehension levels that are too high.

However, it is not unknown for teachers who have not had the experience of working alongside small groups of poor readers to draw up new worksheets which use words that are even longer and more unfamiliar and sentences which are more complex, and for these to be issued when their readability levels are even higher than the original textbooks. The same format is then used week after week. The pupils for whom these support materials were designed become disheartened and bored, and they lose interest.

TEACHING ASSIGNMENT 2

For another of your forthcoming lessons draw up a simplified worksheet that will enable pupils with reading difficulties to:

- locate information more easily
- read the individual words more easily
- grasp the sentence structure
- carry out tasks that relate easily to the pupils' prior knowledge.

FEEDBACK

A more effective worksheet for pupils with learning difficulties may have one or more of the following features:

- it uses sub-headings which enable pupils to locate information
- it breaks the information down into shorter paragraphs
- it highlights the most significant ideas of the original text in the first sentence of each paragraph
- it cuts out lengthy descriptions
- it uses shorter, more familiar words
- it uses shorter, simpler sentences
- it reproduces a wider range of illustrations
- it checks pupil understanding at more frequent intervals
- it discourages copying
- it sets tasks that relate easily to the pupils' prior knowledge.

STRATEGIES FOR DEVELOPING COMPREHENSION ACROSS THE CURRICULUM

An SEN support group, brought together from across the curriculum, can develop a house style for simplified worksheets, so that pupils are used to scanning the sub-headings and lead sentences in order to pick out the main ideas or to seek out answers to specific questions. It would appear that pupils with reading difficulties, just like the most successful readers, rarely fail to make some sense of a demanding text; rather, they find more difficulty locating or updating information. Once they have formed an initial interpretation, they stick to it (APU, 1987).

REFLECTIONS

- What do you do when you have got half-way through an article, and you realize that you have misunderstood some of it? Do you press on regardless or stop and go back?

- How often do you break into the sequence of a text, checking back and skimming forward to ensure understanding?

FEEDBACK

One approach that helps pupils with reading difficulties develop their comprehension skills is to place questions in the midst of a text, which encourages them to qualify their ideas as they read. It could be argued that it is not enough for a teacher to check the readability levels of a text or worksheet before issuing it; there also needs to be a range of tasks which encourage pupils to question and qualify their own first impressions. It is rare, though, for simplified worksheets to hold pupils' attention for long, however patiently they are constructed. Pupils with learning difficulties invariably pick up the social stigma attached to 'easy work' and unless support staff have a fund of variegated resources they eventually reject the help offered.

DISCUSSION OF VARIEGATED STRATEGIES

Support materials do not have to follow the same pattern lesson after lesson. Instead of an introductory text followed by questions, a support teacher can introduce ideas through diagrams or illustrations. Tricia, a history teacher who had joined the SEN support group for a year, produced some excellent work on the Norman Conquest for her group of pupils with physical disabilities and moderate learning difficulties, based on the Bayeux Tapestry. She then found that this could be adapted to form part of an exam for mainstream pupils with reading difficulties.

REFLECTIONS

- How could you introduce pictures or diagrams into simplified worksheets?

FEEDBACK

What Tricia did in this instance was to photocopy some outline drawings of the sequence surrounding Harold's death, and then ask the pupils to comment on what they saw and its significance. The pupils were quick to point out the ambiguity of the arrow in the eye and even to form some judgements about the point of view of the people who created the tapestry.

DISCUSSION OF CLOZE PROCEDURE

The simplified text can be presented with words missing. Pupils then have to use cloze procedure to guess what words should go into the gaps. These missing words can be chosen because they represent the key concepts that the teacher wants to impart. Instead of asking the pupils to answer questions, they are invited to fill in the missing words, then to compose sentences of their own which include them. This can then lead on to lessons which show pupils how to pick out key words in a passage and make their own notes.

TEACHER ASSIGNMENT 3

Draw up a simplified worksheet with missing words for one of your next lessons and share it with your special needs support group.

FEEDBACK

Another teacher in the SEN support group produced a series of simplified science worksheets with missing words on a geology module, using one of the school's computers. At the bottom of the worksheet there was a list of the missing words. The worksheet could be printed off before the lesson and filled in by hand – or left on the wordprocessor, completed as an IT exercise by a couple of pupils and printed off for their science files when completed.

This inspired Polly, an art teacher with strong IT skills in the SEN support group, to produce a set of worksheets on art history using a more powerful computer. She was given the time to produce some interactive programs, which incorporated music, speech and coloured printouts. Other teachers then began looking for commercially produced interactive software in their own subject areas.

DISCUSSION OF MULTIPLE CHOICE

A simplified text can be followed by multiple choice questions. This can be a particularly fruitful approach in subjects like science, where pupils often need to be encouraged to find a logical reason for their answers, or in arts subjects, which encourage interpretation and group discussion. Different support strategies can suggest different pupil groupings. With this approach, pupils with learning difficulties can be encouraged to work alongside their more able peers on more of an equal footing. Pupils with an eclectic or non-conformist cast of mind can find this a particularly stimulating approach – and these may occur at all levels of the ability range.

FEEDBACK

A mixed ability Year 11 English class working on metaphor were set some work on Sylvia Plath's poem 'You're'. This is a complex riddle using apparently easy words about her unborn baby. The poem never refers to it directly but uses images like 'jumping beans' and 'clean slate'. The pupils in the class ranged from Level 10 to the statemented pupil at Level 2. Rather than asking the whole class direct answers with simple answers, it seemed more appropriate to split the class into small discussion groups. The questions were arranged on the page as hints; and there was a list of multiple plausible alternatives. In fact, one of the pupils with very limited ability but of a divergent cast of mind was the first to guess what the poem was about. The class then met as a whole group, with pupils from across the ability range trying to explain why Sylvia Plath should have used ambiguity and such idiosyncratic metaphors to evoke such a universal experience.

DISCUSSION OF GENRE

The same topic can be presented in a range of different forms more appropriate to the learning needs of the pupils concerned. The textbook can be amplified with videos, role-play, the use of newspapers, artefacts, photographs, art, music or story-telling. Many teachers routinely use a variety of approaches, some of which are extremely simple but effective, to hold the interest of a mixed ability class; but unless there is a cross-curricular forum in the school, they do not always share these ideas with teachers who teach different subjects or age groups. The SEN support group can function as a communication channel for the staff as a whole.

TEACHER ASSIGNMENT 4

Bring to your support group of free flow teachers some examples of stimulus material and activities which may enable pupils with learning difficulties greater access to a topic.

FEEDBACK

Following the stress on the use of contemporary texts in the National Curriculum reforms in the study of history, many poor readers who previously enjoyed the subject have found it much more difficult. For a few lessons, it may be helpful to alter the format of the lessons,

telling them stories in modern English. Some lessons on the In-
dustrial Revolution and the slave trade were transformed for one
group when an SEN support teacher presented it as a long-running
historical romance. The hero grew up on one of 'Turnip Townsend's'
farms, ran away to sea and ended up as a cabin boy on a slave ship.
His contemporary, a lad from the West African coast, had been
captured by African traders and sold on to a British 'factory'. The
pupils were invited to help the teacher relate the next part of the epic
as it unfolded week by week, and to research the background.

DISCUSSION OF VARIEGATED TASKS

The task can also be varied. Instead of working on mechanical
exercises with short 'closed' answers, the pupils with learning difficulties can be encouraged to respond with problem solving, some
free writing, a story, role-play, some descriptive writing or a poem.

TEACHING ASSIGNMENT 5

Develop a programme of study for the less able pupils in one of your
classes which includes a wider choice of tasks. You may be surprised
to find that pupils who have a great deal of difficulty applying
themselves to simplified worksheets will respond more happily if
something more creative is demanded.

REFLECTION

- How often have you attempted to use creative or open-ended
  tasks in science, maths or RE with pupils who have special
  needs?

FEEDBACK

Charles was a 16-year-old statemented pupil with coordination
difficulties and a history of autistic-type behaviour. He had 'islands'
of ability even though he could barely read, and he generally func-
tioned at Level 2. When set routine maths exercises, he found
difficulty reaching his target of eight correct sums each lesson, but
when given an investigation, he could solve it more quickly than
teachers with maths degrees. The class was asked to solve a problem
about points on the circumference of a circle and the lines connecting
them.

'If you draw a circle and put one point, how many lines are there?'
'None', said Charles.
'If you put two points and connect them with lines?'
'One.'
'Three points?'
'Three', said Charles.

Charles realized that if you put five points you got ten. He also successfully predicted the number of regions in the circle even though nobody had drawn it for him.

In RE lessons, Charles had tremendous difficulty with copying maps, drawing freehand, answering comprehension questions, filling in gaps in cloze procedure or writing a story. When he completed his Record of Achievement, he reckoned his greatest achievements were in problem solving and writing poems – and this was often how he would make his response to RE lessons. In so doing, he showed unlooked-for understanding of religious characters and the power of ritual:

> *God's call*
>
> Moses was a shepherd
> His sheep ran up God's mountain
> He went to retrieve them
> As he was climbing up,
> He saw an astonishing sight
> A bush that was burning.
> Yet not burning
> He removed his shoes like
> Removing manacles
> God said, 'Go free your kind.'
> Moses dashed down the mountain
> To tell his family about the amazing happenings.

Pupils with difficulties in reading and writing, like Charles, may find school work difficult unless they are given technological aids or personal support. After an extensive project on religious festivals, Charles decided on an imaginative response, though he required one-to-one support from an amanuensis to complete this:

Captain's log – Stardate 25th, time 3 a.m.
I have arrived at a section of Earth called England. I am at a place called Whitehorse Road. I am entering a dwelling called Number Two. I am approaching an entrance. This dwelling has a primitive alarm box. I am using my disarming ray. It was easy to walk through the door without opening it. This is a primitive world where they do not even have matter stabilisers. One of the creatures came down from the upper chambers and I had to use my invisibiliser. He was unable to see me. He ran straight to the alarm box and switched it off. Then he ran into the front chamber, still with his sleeping cover over his head. He

dashed to some strange indoor plant of some kind and began to search through coloured boxes. He pulled out a couple and dragged them in front of a seating item. He started to pull the coloured paper off. A large creature came from the upper chambers and said, 'What time do you call this for a Christmas Day!'

DISCUSSION OF TECHNOLOGY

It would be quite impossible for many pupils to create work that approached their capabilities without the support of computers, computerized spell-checks and dictaphones. It is essential for SEN specialists to work with computer studies teachers, technicians and mainstream subject specialists to ensure these are accessible across the school.

REFLECTIONS

- Is IT available for pupils in all the classrooms of your school?
- Are pupils with special needs able to take laptops or software home?
- Can they access IT at lunch-time?
- Are they given lessons in study skills?

DISCUSSION OF THE USE OF SSA STAFF IN SUPPORT

The most recent recommendations (DES, 1990) suggest a staffing ratio of 10:1 between statemented pupils with learning difficulties or behavioural difficulties and special needs support assistants. Even if a school has rather fewer statemented pupils, it is often extremely useful as well as cost-effective to involve them in a range of support activities, including preparing differentiated materials, offering short-term one-to-one support in areas of the school where integration is problematic, or acting as readers or amanuenses. This will be looked at in greater detail in Chapter 9.

PUPIL PERSPECTIVES

The provision of differentiated materials can become counter-productive, especially if it is handled with insensitivity. When Zia, a non-statemented pupil with language, learning and coordination difficulties, arrived at Eastville School, she could barely read and her writing was slow and laborious.

'Some teachers did not realize I had dyspraxia and they gave me the same work as everyone else. I used to get in moods, especially if it was homework, and it was too hard. [One teacher] always gave me baby work and that was just as bad. Now I can read, it is much easier. Miss still gives me different work in history. We have just been doing something on the Suffragettes. She's very clever about it though. The others don't know it's different. The workbook and worksheets look the same as everyone else's. No one can tell the difference. We have to do course work projects for GCSE. She comes over and asks me what help I need. She's got a lot of extra books and materials. She'll sit down with me and show me how to use them.'

For Louise, a pupil with epilepsy, coordination, language and learning difficulties, the relationship with the teacher and the teacher's communication skills were equally important.

'Some teachers come over to you and explain things properly. It feels OK when they explain things because you know what you're meant to be doing. It is good when they give you a choice, too. It makes it more interesting.'

Brian agreed. He had arrived at Eastville able only to read six words on the Schonell word recognition test, and deeply discouraged.

'My best lesson is textiles, because we always get a choice. I chose to make a Man United pillow, because I knew how I could do it and I wanted to use it. I'm OK in technology because there's not been much reading and writing. I take everything home the moment I finish it – except for my six foot high model of a Spitfire. I wanted it for my roof, but [my partner] wants it too! It makes a difference having a choice, whether you can read or not.'

SUMMARY

Staff who have had little experience of working with small groups of pupils with special needs often find difficulty in producing appropriately differentiated work. A coordinated staffing and inservice strategy can give colleagues more confidence and insight, especially where there is a close match between the skills of the support staff and the pupils' needs. Extra timetabled time for staff to provide in-class support and to prepare additional materials or activities, with the support of the Special Needs Coordinator or LEA learning support services, can make a significant difference in the quality of pupils' learning. Poorly prepared materials can have unforeseen negative consequences, actually reducing low expectations still further.

Effective differentiation can raise attainments and allow greater integration. Support materials, activities and experiences need to be as closely matched to pupils' capabilities as possible, and be interesting and challenging. They need to be introduced with tact and in such a way that the pupils with special needs feel they are being empowered and offered choice. Staff who have had the chance to become involved in a whole-school training programme will have a clearer understanding of the pupils' strengths and weaknesses, their oral and reading abilities, and their prior knowledge of the subject in hand. Where the training programme is incorporated into the school development plan, teachers will also have a better understanding of the way the support materials fit into the overall provision being made through the IEP across the school as a whole, and into the framework of National Curriculum statements of attainment and level descriptors.

The most common form of differentiation is by outcome, though it is difficult to use this approach and reach out effectively to pupils with special needs. The next most common approaches are the simplified worksheet and its mirror image – extension materials. Any single approach can be off-putting in the long run, and the more successful teachers of pupils with special needs keep a variety of strategies and materials in readiness. These range from cloze procedure, multiple choice questions and open-ended tasks to the use of technology and artefacts.

Differentiation is more than a range of approaches. It is an imaginative and creative recognition that all of us are different, that we all learn in different ways and that these means of learning vary over time. Differentiation seeks to surprise children with what they can learn, to make them feel safe to keep learning and to lessen the load of isolation some feel in school.

6

Talented and more able pupils

INTRODUCTION

It may seem unusual to include a discussion of talented and more able pupils in a book on special needs. The Warnock Committee was not encouraged to consider 'procedures for identifying gifted children ... or ... provision for them'. There are no references to the identification or assessment of talented or more able pupils in the Code of Practice. As far as OFSTED are concerned, it seems that such pupils' needs are probably best considered under the aegis of equal opportunities.

The main argument against the inclusion of more able pupils in SEN procedures is that with so many other pressing demands on their time, SENCos will inevitably give their needs too low a priority. It could as well be said of equal opportunities teams, however, that the issue of the most able will always fall a poor third to gender and race. At a practical level, the two issues that are currently at the top of most SENCos' agendas are those that link more able pupils and those with learning difficulties – assessment and differentiation. As the 1995 Annual Report from the Chief Inspector makes clear:

> Weaknesses in assessment procedures often explain weaknesses in provision for both more able pupils and pupils with learning difficulties ... Pupils ... will inevitably fail to realise their potential if teaching ... is directed at a supposed mid point of ability.
>
> (OFSTED, 1995)

In a typical British school, where the proportion of more able pupils gaining high SATs scores or five or more A–Cs at GCSE may be larger than those with learning difficulties, the debate about the way their needs should be defined or who should take responsibility for them is largely academic. But for schools in areas of high social and economic deprivation, there are pressing reasons for reconstructing special provision. In some urban and inner city areas, more than half the pupils may have learning difficulties at some time in their school careers. It is plainly illogical to refer to their needs as *special*. In these areas, it is arguable that the talented and more able pupils constitute the special group.

Under present regulations on parental choice, schools with good reputations for supporting pupils with learning difficulties can be caught in a trap. As they attract more slow learners, they may lose their more able pupils (Ball *et al.*, 1994; Young in Vincent *et al.*, 1995). In these schools, issues like the presentation of special provision and the identification of the more able are being discussed with new urgency. These pupils' success may be vital to the school's survival. Staff who are 'good at' SEN assessment will be motivated to identify more able pupils and to monitor their progress with particular care. SHA (1990) has now recommended that secondary heads should include the more able in SEN assessment procedures:

> Schools must accept that they have a clear duty to such pupils. They should be known to all and their special needs understood. Subject departments ... should set high but realistic new targets for them.

There is a further case for counting the much smaller group of talented pupils who are capable of excelling at music, art, sport or drama or moving beyond the programmes of study appropriate to their Key Stage as 'special', if only because it can be such a drain on any given school's resources to meet their needs adequately. Some LEAs, like Oxfordshire, have even written SEN statements for a tiny sub-group of these pupils to protect their access to individual tuition, 'accelerated' learning and 'enrichment' programmes.

It could be argued that if the competing demands of a market economy for education and high quality provision for the most vulnerable pupils are to be reconciled, special provision may need to be reconstituted. There has always been a case for dropping the term 'special needs'. For many parents and pupils, there is now too much stigma attached to it. Pupils at both extremes of the ability range could now be referred to as 'exceptional' (Francis and Turkington, 1992). The American special education journal *Exceptional Children* includes research on 'gifted' pupils as well as those with learning, behavioural, sensory and physical difficulties. Its founder, Lloyd Dunn (1972), deliberately set out to afford the most able children the same kinds of legal and political protection as pupils with learning difficulties. He also argued that the inclusion of the most able would help reduce the stigma of 'exceptional provision' for those with learning difficulties.

Expectations for the most able have always been criticized by the British Inspectorate. It cannot be assumed that mainstream class-room teachers will know how to identify them or provide appropriate teaching for them without additional support or training. Teachers' concern for these pupils cannot be doubted. This chapter will argue that for SENCos who are creating new whole-school inservice policies for children with learning difficulties in the aftermath of the Code, it can often be a short and popular step to:

- redefine special educational needs
- include consideration of more able pupils in post-Code identification and assessment procedures
- reconstruct special provision to include other groups.

OBJECTIVES

By the end of this chapter, you will have reviewed:

- identification and assessment strategies for talented and more able pupils
- the problem of stigma and the context of differentiation
- a coordinated staffing and training strategy for small-group work, distance learning and individual tuition;

and produced teaching plans for

- differentiated teaching styles, resources and activities
- pupil groupings and individualized learning.

DISCUSSION OF COORDINATED IDENTIFICATION FOR MORE ABLE PUPILS

A sensible starting point for workshops on the identification of talented and more able pupils is to encourage colleagues to explore the range of available strategies. Before the Education Reform Act, it was common for SENCos to screen year groups using norm referenced IQ tests. Since the Cyril Burt controversy, schools have been much more cautious about their reliability and the possibility of ethnic or social class bias. When the National Curriculum was introduced, most survey schools dropped them altogether. Some reserved them for individual pupils with suspected specific learning difficulties or exceptional abilities. As a result, the tests still have a certain mystique about them. All those in common use, such as the NFER, Richmond or Edinburgh tests, have teachers' manuals which include tables indicating the average and 'superior' scores for certain ages. Some schools use norm referenced group reading tests as a rough guide. They are easier to administer but they need to be treated with even greater caution. It can be instructive for colleagues to compare the scores of ex-pupils when they first took these tests with their eventual GCSE or A-level results. The two survey schools that had tried this found a correlation of only 0.36, reinforcing their determination only to use such tests with caution.

Another strategy is to use SAT scores, though there are still doubts about their reliability, both over time and between subjects (TES, 1995). A third is through the teachers' own classroom assessments. One of the problems about using National Curriculum data is that different curricular areas have different definitions. Teachers in the core curriculum, modern languages and humanities have attainment targets to guide them. In the creative arts there are end of Key Stage descriptors. There is still a great deal of work to be done on the moderation of both; this can itself provide a useful starting point for inservice work on assessment for all levels of ability.

Although the definitions and criteria may differ, it can still be fruitful for staff to share their approaches and insights with colleagues from across the curriculum. To the music staff, special gifts can be expressed in instrumental grades. To the PE staff, the criteria can involve achievement in a particular competition or inclusion in a special team. To the drama teacher, it can be assessed through performance. Some researchers and practitioners would also include social skills like leadership in their definitions of exceptional abilities.

The fourth identification strategy is through parental guidance. Parents might know much more than staff about their children's aptitudes – particularly in areas that are not part of the National Curriculum, like skating or chess. And the fifth strategy is to ask the pupils themselves via discussions on their Records of Achievement.

Because of league tables and the pressure on schools to produce high scores at SATs and GCSEs, many mainstream staff are coming together with SENCos and senior managers to identify the pupils who are most likely to benefit from special coaching. Two of the survey schools had set up parents' and pupils' workshops just before revision sessions and had significantly improved their scores. Staff who work together with the pupils and parents in this way not only boost their pupils' attainments but also develop their own abilities to identify the more able.

REFLECTIONS

- What steps does your school take to identify special gifts or abilities?
- How are the particular needs of these children assessed?

- What steps are you taking to stimulate their talents?
- Do you have staff who are happy to mentor such pupils?

FEEDBACK

Some very able pupils will have high attainments in all subjects and they will be easy to identify. Others may go unrecognized without scrupulous identification procedures. Some may have talents, but refuse to show them because of peer pressure. Others may have very specific gifts and yet perform at quite average levels in other areas. Many of the inventions patented by ICI were designed by technical staff rather than PhDs. For a very few children, exceptional talents in one field might even be masked by learning difficulties in others.

Georgiou came to Eastville School from Eastern Europe aged 14 with barely any English. His outstanding abilities in maths and physics might easily have been overlooked without careful assessment and close parental collaboration. He consistently scored top marks in norm referenced and National Curriculum tests in maths and physics. His father said he had been part of a national group for children with special aptitudes in maths. He had also taken part in a national chess team.

He was given E2L lessons in small groups and on an individual basis by the school's special needs staff under the direction of LEA Section 11 staff. He joined a small group of pupils with specific reading difficulties and learned to read English so quickly that he was able to join a mixed ability Key Stage 3 class studying Shakespeare in six weeks. Teaching him how to write English was more problematic. A wide range of teaching strategies was tried, including the most analytical grammar primers. He probably benefited from this in the long term, because his written style became very precise. But he wrote slowly and could only achieve Grade C in English by the age of 16.

Georgiou was given an 'accelerated' course in maths at Eastville. This enabled him to take GCSEs within six months of arriving in this country. In Year 10, he was sent to the local sixth-form college for a few lessons a week. His lecturer designed another 'accelerated' course – in A-level maths and physics. Despite his success in these areas, he had clearly been traumatized by what had happened to him in Romania. He numbered among his closest friends some of the least socially mature and lowest achieving pupils. His attainments outside the core curriculum were extremely variable and many staff found it difficult to get good work from him without special support. He passed only four subjects at Grades A–C and might never have been allowed to take A levels at FE without the accelerated course.

REVIEW OF A COORDINATED STAFFING AND INSERVICE
STRATEGY

So far in this book, we have looked at the deployment of mainstream
teaching staff in special provision for pupils with learning difficulties. This strategy can also be used as a way of enabling class and
subject teachers to develop their teaching skills with the more able.
Year by year, the staff who have opted to spend a few lessons every
week teaching pupils with learning difficulties their basic skills and
then producing differentiated materials for them and supporting
them in mainstream classes, can also be enabled to spend a few
lessons every week for a term working with small groups of talented
and more able pupils. They can also become 'mentors' to these
pupils, counselling them about their work or helping them with their
Records of Achievement. Staff with special interests and skills can be
matched with pupils who have gifts in those areas. This can ensure
that a number of staff get a chance to explore what can be done to
raise expectations and thus continue to change the ecology of the
school.

In the same way that some of the staff involved in teaching basic
literacy to less able pupils spontaneously set to work, revising
teaching materials and developing differentiated activities in order
to involve these pupils in their mainstream lessons, some of those
who have had the chance to work with the most able immediately
start to produce extension and distance learning materials. Other
staff benefit from inservice courses on the needs of the more able and
talented. In schools like Eastville, staff who have been timetabled to
provide in-class support for one year know that they will have the
chance to spend some of that time working with small groups of the
most able. Given the complexities and very specific demands of the
National Curriculum, it is far more effective for subject teachers to
provide differentiated materials and activities for the most able
within their own departments than for a generalist gifted pupils'
mentor to do so.

Through the development of individual counselling and small
group work with the most able, the SENCo can begin to delegate
special provision for the more able to a range of staff across the
curriculum, who are expert at their own subjects, as well as more
sensitive to the needs of these pupils. Subject specialists who are
most aware of the structure of the National Curriculum in their own
subjects will again act as agents of change for the school as a
whole.

As the Chief Inspector's Annual Report (OFSTED, 1995) makes
clear, streaming is no guarantee that the more able will receive
appropriate work, 'if, when pupils are organised into sets, one set is

given much the same work as another'. A coordinated staffing and training strategy can also act as a way of creating *ad hoc* networks of concerned teachers who will spearhead the raising of expectations. A few of the lessons of volunteer support staff can be given over to producing differentiated materials on a similar basis to that described in Chapter 5. Other lessons can be allocated to enrichment in higher order study skills (Feuerstein, 1980; Blagg *et al.*, 1988) or accelerated learning. The SENCo can be contracted to work more closely with those departments for that year and either provide inservice training in the ways outlined below or organize others to do it.

REFLECTIONS

- How much time is available in your school for mainstream staff to prepare a range of differentiated materials and activities for the most able pupils?
- How does your Special Needs Coordinator enable staff to develop their range of resources for the most able?

FEEDBACK

One of the staff in the survey schools was a noted local historian. Given the chance to work with a small group of more able pupils, he produced a range of new materials on a Victorian theatre, which was used thereafter as a special project for able pupils in mixed ability mainstream classes. Another had close links with a group of local artists and these were enabled to work with exceptional pupils for blocks of time as 'artists in residence'.

DISCUSSION OF STIGMA AND THE CONTEXT OF DIFFERENTIATION

For some pupils in some schools, special talents and outstanding ability can become a stigma. They can be made to feel isolated, particularly if their teachers give them completely different work or regularly single out their work for praise. Those with good social skills learn to cope and keep their friendships in good repair. But life can be difficult for those without everyday interpersonal skills. They can be teased, put under pressure from their peers to slow down their work rate, use simpler vocabulary, hide their more original ideas, or disguise their enthusiasms.

Most very able pupils can cope well enough with peer pressure, but a few succumb to internal pressure. They need always to excel, never to risk failure. The problem can be exacerbated if they are 'convergent' thinkers and if staff only set 'closed exercises' rather than a range of exploratory tasks. In such classrooms, the pressure to achieve may bring its own frustrations, the only gesture towards differentiation to be given what one more able pupil described as 'more examples to complete while the rest of the class finish off'.

More able pupils have different learning styles, as do the broad majority of their peers. Some write easily and fluently. They may flourish in classes where staff use a graduated range of tasks, with less demanding, closed questions at the start and more stimulating open questions at the end of a project. Others prefer to think more deeply and write more slowly. These pupils might never get to the 'harder' work. Some are independent learners and enjoy the opportunity to use the library to soak up new information on their own topics, especially if they have been shown how to use a wide range of study skills. Others are more motivated to reflect and analyse. They will set themselves original problems, and enjoy the opportunity to solve them at the computer or in the workshop. Some are more passive learners, only feeling secure when given clearly designated tasks and working on them under close direction from a teacher.

Differentiation has its pitfalls for able pupils, just as it does for the less able, and it can prove counter-productive unless the teacher understands:

- the pupils' prior knowledge
- the pupils' particular strengths
- what approaches help motivate which pupils
- what makes pupils feel threatened or isolated
- what makes them feel able to explore and develop
- how to win and retain their trust
- how all this fits into the demands of the National Curriculum;

or if the materials are:

- ill-matched to the pupils' abilities
- insufficiently interesting or challenging
- presented in such a way that makes the users feel cut off from their peer group.

The content of the materials and activities and the context in which they are presented can help staff to reach out more forcefully to exceptional pupils – or reinforce boredom and low expectations.

REFLECTIONS

- Do staff in your school plan their 'chalk and talk' lessons so that they use a mixture of straightforward and more demanding questions?
- How do they enable the most able to develop their ideas in whole-class, small-group and paired discussions?
- How do they help them to cope with positive criticism?
- Are the readability levels of the extension materials in your school ever checked against the most able pupils' reading ages?
- Are their conceptual levels checked against the most able pupils' abilities?
- Are the extension tasks checked against the relevant National Curriculum level descriptions?
- How wide is the range of pupil activities offered?
- How much choice is built into the provision of differentiated materials?

FEEDBACK

Alan was a quiet, introverted pupil who felt the pressures from his peer group particularly acutely. He believed there was a minority in most of his classes who did not want to work. Most of his teachers spent much of their time with those pupils, encouraging them, nagging them and negotiating an acceptable minimum. If he or anyone else in the class produced more, he felt under pressure from these pupils to slow down. If he was really drawn into some project, and produced work of a good standard, some teachers would be so excited that they would give him much harder tasks. A really difficult piece of extension work out of the blue could be really discouraging. It not only made him feel different from the rest of the class, it could also rob him of his enthusiasm.

What Alan wanted was a greater degree of understanding and sensitivity from his teachers in terms of his personal abilities, the subjects and the everyday pressures of classroom life. His art teacher, Mr Green, was someone who made him feel this. Alan had been working on a demanding painting for some time. When Mr Green had seen the initial sketches in the artroom, he had said they were good but he 'did not make anything big out of it'. He discussed the main strengths in the drawing and then he showed him another approach which would help with the colour.

When Alan finished the line drawing he was really pleased with it, but the colouring seemed to spoil it – until right at the end. That had made him feel pleased he had spent so long on this picture. It had been Mr Green's idea to work in that way but Alan would not have followed his suggestions if he had not trusted him. This very positive result had encouraged him to do a lot more art work at home on his own initiative.

DISCUSSION OF DIFFERENTIATION BY OUTCOME

One of the commonest teaching strategies is differentiation by outcome, but it is one of the most difficult to manage effectively for more or less able pupils. It tends to encourage the fastest workers, and though these often include the cleverest, this may not always be so. Clever but slow writers may feel under-stimulated and become discouraged. As part of a programme of inservice training, designed to increase understanding of Stage 1 of the Code of Practice, staff from Southville, one of the project schools, designed a range of teaching assignments for specific pupils with exceptional abilities in mixed ability classes. Most staff chose differentiation by outcome for their assignment.

INSET TEACHING ASSIGNMENT 1

For one of the lessons you are planning to teach in the next week, design a piece of work that is differentiated by outcome. Try to ensure that:

- your introductions to the lessons contain a mixture of unfamiliar words and concepts, unusual examples and open questions
- the class groupings allow the most able to work together for some topics
- the readability levels of the extension materials are equivalent to the most able pupils' reading ages
- their conceptual levels are appropriate for the most able pupils
- the tasks reflect the relevant National Curriculum levels
- there is a degree of choice.

FEEDBACK

At Southville School, the head of the modern languages department invited the LEA advisory teacher into the school to produce extension materials as part of departmental INSET on differentiation. They started with speaking and listening exercises – buying food for a party. The task was split into core and extension activities. The core included recognizing items of food and short phrases related to liking and buying, and being able to use them when replying to the teacher (AT 1 and 2: Levels 1 and 2). The extension activities (AT 1 and 2: Level 4) included being able to recognize longer extracts from the dialogues they had practised the previous week and to prepare presentations with whole sentences from them. This workshop was followed up with an invitation to A-level students and their French-speaking assistants from the local sixth-form college to come to Southville School to work with small groups of more able pupils for one afternoon a week for one term. In-class support in modern languages was rearranged with the SENCo's help and the pupils made significant progress.

DISCUSSION OF STUDY SKILLS

On a whole-school study day on differentiation at Southville School, the second most popular choice was an assignment on study skills for the more able. It is all too easy to assume that these pupils can be sent to a library to work on a project without being first shown how to access books, use indexes, skim, scan, take notes, precis or produce their own written material in their own words. Pupils who are extremely conversant with computers may still type with two fingers. They may not know how to use a spread sheet or how to edit text.

INSET TEACHING ASSIGNMENT 2

Design a project for a more able pupil which relates to the pupil's special interests and prior knowledge that will enable him/her to:

- locate information in textbooks and encyclopedias, using the table of contents and the index
- pick out the topic of a given paragraph in a limited period of time
- locate and list the keywords and concepts
- list facts and data from the text that provide evidence for each of these keywords
- produce a summary of the information in their own words, which includes the pupil's own drawings and photocopied illustrations, using a word processor and a desk-top publisher.

FEEDBACK

Projects can employ fictional sources as well as non-fiction. The English department at Southville decided to bring a writer of teenage novels into school, encourage pupils to read his books and then produce their own pastiches of his work. This was co-funded by the school. As a result, a teacher with particular concerns with the more able persuaded three Year 9 pupils to collaborate on a science fiction novel in a very similar style, starting off during lessons and then staying late after school. They used the school's word processors, handing in the disks each night to be printed, discussing the latest draft with their teacher during the day and re-editing the next evening. The IT technician also showed them how to design the graphics for the cover and their own illustrations and the pupils then sent the finished versions off to the writer for his comments.

Some gifted pupils with a flair for mimicry will, given the chance, enjoy writing in the style of different novelists or poets. A special seminar with their mentor, exploring some of Keats' *Odes* and then composing a pastiche can help deepen their love of literature. Talented pupils as young as Key Stage 2 might also enjoy constructing their own versions of historical texts. Others may prefer free writing, a story, role-play, some descriptive writing or a poem instead of an essay.

Other projects might encourage pupils to design their own experiments in science or to juggle a range of variables. Pupils with high ability can find 'cognitive dissonance' particularly motivating. The mentor can present the pupil with two mutually contradictory explanations for a scientific finding for the pupil to find another hypothesis which can resolve them. Nuffield Science and the CASE materials have done this in a structured way to help develop 'thinking skills'.

PUPIL PERSPECTIVES

Karen performed well in most subjects. Her attendance was poor in Year 9.

> 'Sometimes I can get bored, because I finish the work quickly and there's nothing else to do. In [one subject] I do the same work over and over again each year. In the end you feel I can't be bothered, if the teachers can't.
>
> 'Differentiation can be helpful. In [another subject] you are told what you need to know to get good grades in the exam. My teacher told me, "I've got some extension work for you Karen. Would you mind doing it?" I suppose I was a bit cross because of the extra work I had to do – but also proud because I'd been singled out. I would not have done it for any teacher, but I get on all right with [her]. Some of the kids called me a swot, but I just ignored them or said something back.'

Kate agreed.

'You get called all the time, but it has never bothered me. I just laugh it off or make a joke. The other kids don't really mind because they know that Karen and I are capable of doing extra work. Miss sets the work for the whole class, then she gives us the extension work. She always looks through your work with you and suggests ways of developing your ideas.'

Alan said:

'Other teachers get it wrong sometimes just by trying too hard. They provide extension work, but it can just be too hard. That can put you off, because you're supposed to be able to do harder work and you don't want to let them down. Some of the best teachers know how to explain things well and get you to work harder without you ever realizing.'

SUMMARY

There has been growing concern among some mainstream teachers and SENCos about the special needs of more able and talented pupils. The Warnock Committee was discouraged from looking at this group and in most schools responsibility for their progress is seen as an equal opportunities issue. However, as OFSTED have made plain, their problems are very similar to those of pupils with learning difficulties – low expectations, poor identification and assessment and a lack of differentiation.

Some schools have begun to reconstruct special provision so that it more closely matches the needs of their schools. They have included the more able in their staged SEN assessment procedures. Southville School said that one of the main reasons why they chose a specific group reading test was that it screened out the less able but also indicated which of their 11-year-olds also had reading ages of 16 or more. Some LEAs are also considering redefining special provision to include the more able and gifted. The American term 'exceptional children' has been used to give special provision for children at both extremes of the ability range a more positive cachet.

A coordinated staffing and training programme can be set up to raise the attainments of the most able. Some staff need little support to identify the special needs of these pupils and to provide their own extension materials. Others prefer extra timetabled time to prepare additional materials or activities with the guidance of the Special Needs Coordinator, the Equal Opportunities Coordinator or LEA support services. It could be argued that staff need the opportunity to develop ideas and materials in a non-threatening situation, working with pupils they like on topics they enjoy. Poorly prepared materials can also have negative consequences, driving down more able pupils' expectations.

Differentiated materials need to be interesting, challenging and closely matched to the pupils' abilities. They need to be introduced in such a way that the pupils appreciate they are being empowered and offered choice. The teacher also has to have a clear idea of the way in which the materials fit into the framework of National Curriculum statements of attainment and level descriptors. The most common form of differentiation is by outcome, though it is difficult to use this approach and to reach out effectively to pupils at either extreme of the ability range. The next most common approaches are extension materials and accelerated learning. Some schools have been trying special courses in thinking skills and study skills for the most able. According to some students, special teaching strategies were only as effective as the communication skills or the day-to-day organization of the teachers themselves. Some staff appear to have had little understanding of peer pressure, even showing pupils up in front of their friends. They misjudged what pupils were capable of and dampened enthusiasms they intended to awaken. Staff needed more time to learn the necessary skills.

Other staff made pupils feel as if they always expected them to do well. They knew how to listen to a group of pupils and to make an individual response to each. This did not always have to be positive or encouraging. It could include criticism, which would be accepted if it was realistic and introduced in an atmosphere of mutual respect. The most subtle classroom management would make the more able feel it was safe to continue to learn and lessen the sense of isolation some shared with those pupils who had learning or behavioural difficulties.

7

Emotional and behavioural difficulties

INTRODUCTION

Since the publication of the Draft Code of Practice, there has been a lively debate in many schools about the responsibilities of the Special Needs Coordinator in identifying and assessing pupils with behavioural and emotional difficulties. In some of the survey schools, SENCos have worked in close collaboration with pastoral staff and senior managers on prevention, planning and provision for these pupils (Bell and Best, 1988). They have played their part in promoting greater consistency in the management of troubled and challenging behaviour and in reviewing the development of skills needed by mainstream classroom teachers.

Many other SENCos have concentrated their attention on mainstream pupils with learning difficulties and statemented pupils, however. Provision for mainstream pupils with emotional or behavioural difficulties would be seen as quite separate – the province of secondary pastoral staff or the senior management in primary schools. In these schools, behavioural policies have focused on prevention, discipline, rewards and sanctions rather than on the assessment of individuals with behavioural difficulties or meeting their educational needs.

The SEN Code of Practice is less than explicit about these issues. There are many references to 'the child's behaviour', 'factors contributing to any difficulty' and 'pastoral care' in its chapter on school-based assessment. It is only in chapter 3, on statutory assessment, that it clarifies its position. These pupils could be seen as having learning difficulties as defined in the 1993 Act, because 'They may fail to meet expectations in school and in some but by no means all cases may disrupt the education of others'.

What this chapter will argue is that as each school reinterprets the Code in terms of its own needs and concerns, many more will find that it makes sense for SENCos to work in closer collaboration with the pastoral team or the senior staff. This can be a delicate matter, given the higher status of pastoral management in many schools. But it is quite clear that SENCos have a role to play in reviewing whole-school policies and procedures on behavioural management and pastoral care in the light of the SEN Code. What makes this all the more urgent is that, since the publication of the Code, many LEAs have made the input of its outside agencies, such as behaviour support services or Educational Psychologists, conditional on their being actively consulted about individual education plans. In such authorities, headteachers will undoubtedly want SENCos to work more closely with senior managers and pastoral staff on these pupils' IEPs.

OBJECTIVES

This chapter aims to:

- review the development of whole-school policies on behaviour and pastoral care in the light of the SEN Code
- explore ways of promoting greater consistency in the management of troubled and challenging behaviour
- review the development of skills needed by mainstream classroom teachers in dealing with emotional and behavioural difficulties
- examine procedures for the identification, assessment and support of pupils with emotional and behavioural difficulties
- examine the development of IEPs for individual pupils with emotional or behavioural difficulties.

DISCUSSION OF WHOLE-SCHOOL POLICIES

Many heads and teachers have come to recognize the effect that recent social and economic changes have had on their more demanding pupils. Factors such as unemployment, insecure employment, low pay, child poverty and the growth of single-parent families appear to interact. It has been claimed by Rutter and Smith (1995), for example, that while recent changes in family structures have had detrimental effects on the emotional and intellectual development of all children, those from poor families can be much more vulnerable. It has also been argued that school leavers with few educational qualifications in areas of high unemployment have less to aim for – in terms both of getting a job and of family commitments – and that boys in particular who grow up in such areas have fewer positive male role models. It is indisputable that exclusion rates from schools have risen, the crime rate has increased and more young men are being sent to prison.

At the same time, market researchers have noticed a shift in values among young people in the 1990s. Typical of this was a 1994 MORI poll of 15–35-year-olds, which concluded that two-thirds felt their generation was experiencing a 'moral crisis'. When questioned about the Ten Commandments for the poll, a majority could only recall three. Injunctions such as 'Thou shalt not drink and drive' were considered more relevant than traditional values. Schools were not blamed for this by the young people, however; they were singled out as the places which set the best example and where people learned most about the difference between right and wrong. Schools can and do make a difference, as the Elton Report (DES, 1989a) on *Discipline in Schools* claimed:

> When we visited schools we were struck by the differences in their feel and atmosphere. Our conversations with teachers left us convinced that some schools have a more positive atmosphere than others. . . . We found that we could not explain these different school atmospheres by saying that the pupils came from different home backgrounds. Almost all the schools we visited were in what many teachers would describe as difficult urban areas. We had to conclude that these differences had something to do with what went on in the schools themselves.

Elton argued that there was a 'continuum' of behavioural difficulties in school. Many children undergo periods of emotional stress at some time, or they like to test out the boundaries to what is permissible. The majority of disciplinary problems experienced by teachers are relatively minor, like pupils talking out of turn. The cumulative effects of these minor problems make them the most wearing for staff to deal with, however, and unless they were dealt with consistently, more serious problems could result. It was clear to the Committee that instances of challenging behaviour had to be seen in the context of each school's general ethos. Their response, and one that was in line with the government's policy of more locally devolved management for schools, was that individual heads and governors should formulate their own behavioural and pastoral policies which would be specific to the school. The Elton Report suggested that many such policies would include:

- a general statement of principles and values
- a clear set of rules for pupils
- staff guidelines
- a list of sanctions
- a list of rewards.

REFLECTIONS

- Does your school have a behaviour policy covering the main Elton Report recommendations?
- In your school, was there an opportunity for all staff, including those with SEN responsibilities, to be consulted about behavioural policies?
- How were parents and governors involved?
- How were pupils involved?
- Did pupils with emotional or behavioural difficulties join in?

FEEDBACK

All the schools featured in this LEA's survey into the moderation of the SEN Code of Practice had a behavioural code, though the input from the special needs team varied. At Eastville, the policy was initially drafted by an *ad hoc* group of eight volunteer teachers, which was chaired by the SENCo. It included a senior manager, heads of department, pastoral and special needs post-holders, other middle managers and newly qualified teachers. The advisory group also represented the range of staffroom opinion, from the most conservative to the most liberal. Long before the SEN Code was published, it was thought that the development of a behavioural policy could help prevent learning difficulties. Some researcher/ practitioners are now suggesting that policy development and review could be seen as part of a hypothetical Stage Zero, the necessary precursor to the identification and assessment of behavioural difficulties within the SEN Code.

The Eastville policy group sub-divided into four pairs, which looked at general principles, rules for pupils, staff guidelines and rewards and sanctions. The pair who looked at rules for pupils invited their classes to draw up their own school rules, and the most representative were read out in assembly. The Special Needs Co-ordinator also asked some of the most challenging pupils for their comments. One might expect that behavioural rules would be so subjective that everyone would have their own views. Interestingly enough, there was a high degree of consensus among the pupils. Even the most disturbed children accepted both that there had to be rules and that those that appeared to be the most representative were acceptable to them.

It could be argued that for any given school, a degree of shared understanding may exist at an implicit level. Theoretical sociologists, like Schutz (1964), would refer to these unspoken understandings as examples of 'inter-subjectivity'. If this is so, it would follow that the job of those who write the disciplinary code is not to impose their own ideas on the school but to listen to and articulate these inter-subjective understandings. School rules that grow out of implicit habits and patterns of thinking are most likely to command respect. What would be right for one community would not necessarily be right for another. It was certainly true that schools in the survey had different sets of rules and that specific kinds of rule-breaking elicited stronger feelings in some schools than in others.

At Eastville, all the sub-groups' initial drafts were circulated for comments from individual members, then the whole group met again to draw the policy together. They were joined by the Eastville chair of governors and a parent governor. At a specially convened staff meeting, the staff as a whole were asked to make their own comments, suggestions and amendments. A special parents' meeting was also called. Fifty parents turned up and went through the same process. Finally, the revised policy went back to the full governing body, where the Code was agreed with only minor amendments.

MANAGEMENT TASK 1

If the head, senior management team and governing body accept that the identification and assessment of behavioural difficulties are to be included in the new staged SEN procedures, it might be helpful if a representative group of staff could be called together to review the school's behavioural policy. It may be possible to involve pupils, parents and individual governors. In this way, there can be clear agreement about the detailed issues thrown up by the various stages in the assessment procedure, such as what kinds of behaviours staff can expect to deal with in their own classrooms, which ones should be notified to others in school, which ones they can expect school-based help with and which ones would be discussed with outside agencies.

DISCUSSION OF CONSISTENCY

As many schools have found, there is a difference between drawing up a disciplinary code and ensuring that it is implemented by all staff in a consistent manner. Pupils quickly find out the way that different staff define unacceptable behaviour in their classrooms, or even how their degree of tolerance shifts from day to day. As one teacher put it,

'On a good day, when I'm in a good mood, I'll let things go. The lesson is going well. Why should I pull it up because someone forgot themselves and swore at another pupil? On a bad day, though, I'll go mad at the same thing. The kids don't know where they stand!'

Schools in the survey, which employed a corporate approach to discipline, appreciated the benefits. Once the broad principles have been discussed and digested, the practical details need to be agreed. If there is agreement that there should be a 'No swearing' rule, staff and pupils will also need to be clear about what constituted the bottom line, what their rights and responsibilities were and how they could expect rule-breaking to be dealt with.

REFLECTIONS

- Have staff in your school had the opportunity to look at their rights as teachers?
- Have they reviewed the pupils' rights?
- Have they reviewed their own and the pupils' responsibilities?

FEEDBACK

At a professional training day on the identification and assessment of behavioural difficulties, staff at Eastville School began by compiling a list of their own worst fears. Was there anything that made them dread coming to school on a Monday morning? This led to small group discussions about the issues of teachers' rights and responsibilities and pupils' rights and responsibilities. Having started with their major concerns for themselves and for the children, they then tried to deduce rules from them.

Given the large number of children with mobility difficulties in the school, the staff had decided in principle that there should be 'No running or pushing' in the corridors. This apparently simple rule had extensive implications. It was difficult for pupils not to push if they were jammed into narrow corridors at change of lessons. However, if they were encouraged to use the full range of school entrances and exits, this would relieve the pressure. All class registration staff would need to tell pupils which way to go during the day.

Pupils had the right to feel safe and this would only come with effective corridor supervision at lesson changeovers. This in turn meant that class teachers had to play their part in packing up a few moments before the bell and escorting pupils out of and into their classrooms. Senior members of staff on non-contact time should be timetabled to clear the corridors. Pastoral heads and heads of department on non-contact time should clear their own areas.

The staff also decided that they had the right not to be subjected to pupils' swearing. On reflection, they agreed that all swearing, however apparently innocuous, should be challenged by teachers in their own classrooms. Swearing would be seen as a fundamental issue in the school. Pupils who swore would be reported to their form tutors. If a pattern of swearing emerged, this would be seen as worthy of reporting at Level 1 of the SEN Code. However, the staff also felt that there was a difference between pupils who let swear-words drop and then made an immediate apology, and those who used swear-words aggressively towards another individual. In these more serious cases, the staff felt that pupils should know that other staff and their parents would be informed. This could be seen as a Stage 2 issue. Pupils swearing deliberately and aggressively at another person, particularly a member of staff, could also be liable to temporary exclusion. This school felt they owed it to the whole school community – and the pupils with behavioural difficulties – not to turn a blind eye.

MANAGEMENT TASK 2

If the head, senior management team and governing body accept that the identification and assessment of behavioural difficulties are to be included in the new staged SEN procedures, it might be helpful to decide how the school development plan and inservice programme need to be updated.

DISCUSSION OF PUPIL MANAGEMENT SKILLS

Enforcing school rules and forestalling the pupils' challenges to them are among the most demanding aspects of teaching. In order to prevent difficult behaviour, it helps to know the most difficult pupils and to anticipate their moods and actions. They need a clear and accepted set of rules and staff have to be able to keep on asserting themselves. There is a range of skills packages which schools can arrange for the whole staff or interested individuals to learn, some of which will help staff to manage minor disruption more confidently, others which will deal with more complex and serious issues:

- alcohol and drug education
- assertion
- assertive discipline
- attendance
- behaviour modification
- bullying

- child protection
- crisis management
- eating disorders
- preventing classroom disruption.

REFLECTIONS

- Is there an opportunity for individual and small groups of staff to attend taster or full-scale courses in the skills of pupil management?
- Is there a programme of support for new staff and staff who are experiencing difficulties in managing challenging behaviour at your school?
- Is there a programme of staff development for the whole staff?

FEEDBACK

Two of the survey schools had opted for the full twelve-hour Assertive Discipline training package (Canter, 1992), as part of their staff development. Having carried out a review of their disciplinary policies in the aftermath of the Elton Report, they already had a working set of Principles, Rules, Rewards and Consequences, but they felt they needed greater consistency, a more affirmative approach and a scheme which could be tied more closely into the individual target setting fundamental to the Code of Practice. Both the secondary and primary schools involved found that the focus on regular rewards and recognition for positive behaviour had a marked effect on the ethos of the school. Pupils with more severe emotional and behavioural difficulties responded positively to the praise and recognition and to the peer pressure from their classmates. When individual education plans were drawn up for these pupils, they now referred to the actual rules they were breaking most frequently in their list of targets.

DISCUSSION OF GRADUATED RESPONSES TO EMOTIONAL AND BEHAVIOURAL DIFFICULTIES

In order to maintain a calm and orderly learning environment, schools have to be able to identify troublesome behaviour and to manage it promptly and effectively. It can also help if pupils know that the staff are consistent about infringements of the school rules. Teachers' confidence can grow if they are used to working collaboratively in a blame-free environment and have a graduated set of management strategies to back them up.

REFLECTIONS

- Does your school have back-up systems in place for all staff which enable them to deal promptly with disruption?
- How easily can the staff be kept informed about troubled and troublesome pupils?
- Does your school listen to all sides when an incident has occurred, including that of the difficult child and the parent?

FEEDBACK

Many of the survey schools had developed a range of collaboratively staffed back-up systems to enable classroom teachers to deal promptly and effectively with classroom disruption, from the minor to the most extreme incident. An inner city primary school, like Southville, had a 'network', which enabled staff to move pupils out of their own classrooms into those of a neighbour for short periods. Southville employed a sophisticated identification and assessment pattern, based on their own behavioural policy. Any pupil who had a pattern of removal on the network was seen as needing support at Stage 2 of the SEN Code. The staff had undertaken a whole-school training package in assertive discipline, and they had lists of basic rules in every classroom so that pupils knew where the bottom line was.

At Eastville, an urban comprehensive, there was a series of support and disciplinary tiers. The first tier, which was designed to help colleagues deal with 'causes for concern', would entail advice and follow up from the head of department. The second tier would involve pupils being sent out of a class for a single lesson on a 'cooperative system'. This would ensure that pupils causing more disruptive problems could be sent to work with a colleague in another part of the school. Staff would join the system on a voluntary basis, offering to take disruptive pupils from other colleagues at a time when they had particularly settled classes.

In order to deal proactively with more challenging problems, there was a third tier of senior staff who were timetabled to act as 'duty tutors' during non-contact time. Such staff would start their duty tutor lessons by patrolling the school, settling late-comers into lessons and ensuring there was no internal truancy. Staff knew they could then be contacted in the duty tutor office.

Following recent traumatic events, such as the 1994 stabbing of a pupil at Hallgarth School, Eastville also employed an additional tier – the 'crisis management team'. The senior management team had brainstormed a list of potential crisis scenarios. Staff had been given distinctive roles – specific secretaries detailed to assemble the crisis team and to contact external services, designated senior managers to handle the actual crisis, other designated staff ready to take pupils to hospital, others to contact parents, others to work with distressed children and another to operate the cover arrangements. There were plans to keep all the relevant staff and external agencies informed and there were contact numbers for longer-term counselling. The aim of all these back-up systems was to minimize disruption to class work and to maintain an atmosphere of calm, no matter what challenges pupils and staff were facing.

In urban schools like Eastville, disciplinary incidents continue to occur, despite all the Stage Zero preparatory and preventive work. When they did, there were standard procedures, which the school hoped would exemplify the spirit of the Children Act and the SEN Code. The pupil who had broken the rules would be given the opportunity to put his or her point of view, in writing wherever possible. Where there were conflicting opinions about what actually happened, the pupils could be asked to nominate their own 'witnesses', who would also be asked to write their own 'statements'. Whenever parents were contacted about disciplinary problems, they would be encouraged to put their point of view. The main point in collecting information from all these people was to ensure that though the school would not accept disruptive behaviour, it would always be seen to be trustworthy, above-board and even-handed in its dealings with the pupils responsible.

The staff would also be encouraged to keep their own observations about troubled or troublesome behaviour as objective, factual and specific as possible. There were special staff pro formas, reflecting the school rules, which readily lent themselves to the school's special needs identification and assessment procedures and which would allow for comments from the pupils, their witnesses, their parents, the staff concerned, the back-up staff, the cooperative system, duty tutor or crisis team as appropriate.

DISCUSSION OF A STAGED APPROACH TO THE IDENTIFICATION AND ASSESSMENT OF EMOTIONAL AND BEHAVIOURAL DIFFICULTIES

As the 1986 Education Act reminds us, it is the first duty of a school to secure an acceptable standard of pupil behaviour. Overcoming the learning difficulties of pupils with emotional and behavioural problem is, as the SEN Code of Practice suggests, secondary. The Code introduces another set of priorities, like building trust and rapport with the demanding pupils and their parents, understanding the causes of their problems and inculcating self-discipline. Effective identification and assessment procedures have to combine prompt and decisive action with thorough observation, exploration and discussion.

While it is comparatively easy to screen out reading difficulties, or to form an objective assessment of physical disabilities, this is much more problematic for emotional and behavioural problems. Children behave differently at home and at school, and pupils with apparently similar problems – such as inability to work in groups – seem to react very differently in different classrooms. It would also appear that some short-term identification strategies might label pupils. The way in which schools assess troubled and troublesome pupils may be crucial for both the school and the individuals concerned.

As Elton suggests (DES, 1989a), many pupils have short-term emotional or behavioural difficulties. In an urban school like East-ville, as many as half the pupils in some year groups are referred to the Stage 1 special needs meetings at some time in their school careers because of difficult or disruptive behaviour, underachieve-ment related to emotional difficulties, attendance problems or prob-lems with relationships. The action plans for such pupils will mainly involve a period of support and monitoring from the class or year tutor. Stage 1 action plans can form the basis of IEPs and provide a positive learning experience for many pupils.

In a caring school, staff will want to be alert to the first signs of distress or disruption , exploring the nature of the difficulty with the pupil, contacting the parents as appropriate and discussing possible solutions with other members of staff. If the problem seems to be related to the curriculum, arrangements can be made to foster greater differentiation, according to ability or learning style. The Stage 1 meetings will harness the concerns and expertise of the staff as a whole.

REFLECTIONS

- Do the staff in your school have a regular opportunity to discuss the special needs of pupils with short-term behavioural or emo-tional difficulties?
- How have they responded to the changing patterns of family life, employment and childhood poverty on pupil learning?
- Do they feel they have had appropriate support from their col-leagues or members of outside agencies?

FEEDBACK

There has been increasing concern among Special Needs Coordinators in the survey schools about the incidence of classroom disruption and distress and its effect on pupil learning. In a recent evaluation meeting at Eastville School, the SENCo and pastoral staff reviewed the proportion of pupils in Year 11 who had shown troubled and troublesome behaviour at some time in their school lives, the apparent cause and severity of their problems and the kinds of support they had been given by the school and outside agencies.

The group looked at the records of the 40 pupils who had finished their careers in the bottom band for maths, in terms of their learning difficulties, their emotional and behavioural difficulties and the degree of interaction between them. These pupils were taught in two parallel groups. As well as their mainstream maths teacher, these classes had also had periods of intensive support from staff from other departments. These programmes of support had been designed as part of a coordinated staffing and inservice strategy, assisting individual pupils with basic numeracy and providing experientially based training for the staff. Geography teachers helped with lessons about coordinates, for instance, and learned how pupils with difficulties in maths coped with a skill that was common to both subjects.

Before the review of these 40 bottom band pupils began, there was discussion about the relationship between learning and behavioural difficulties. It was expected that a sub-set of these less able pupils would have experienced emotional or behavioural difficulties, which were directly traceable to their learning difficulties. It can be extremely frustrating to realize that no matter how hard you try, you will always remain in the bottom set, that you will be entered for the lowest tier of exams or none at all – and that this will have harmed your prospects of a job.

The meeting also assumed that there would be another sub-group of pupils whose difficulties were traceable to their family problems. There would be a third sub-group with medical or sensory difficulties affecting both learning and behaviour. And there would be a fourth sub-group from settled homes, with parents in employment, who were behaving well, working positively and achieving well, albeit at a low level.

However, when the evaluation meeting began their analysis of the individual pupils in this bottom maths band, they found that only one out of the 40 pupils fitted this last category. Three had medical and sensory difficulties – epilepsy, moderate hearing loss – and one had perceptual problems related to specific learning difficulties. The proportion with social or familial problems was much higher than expected. Twenty-six pupils out of the 40 had committed offences leading to a court report; 30 came from families which were or had been headed by a single parent; and 32 out of 40 – or 80 per cent – had registered for free school meals.

A few case histories would help clarify the special needs of this bottom maths band, most of whom Eastville School had been able to support at Stage 1 of the identification and assessment process or to refer on for school-based support at Stage 2, or school-based support, with advice and input from external agencies at Stage 3.

CASE HISTORIES

- *Albert* is a pleasant, hard-working pupil, attaining at Level 3/4 in maths, who comes to school every day and never disrupts lessons. He required in-class differentiation especially for algebra and data.
- *Bonnie* has well-controlled epilepsy with occasional absences and minor tantrums. She has had considerable support from her teachers and GP. She was registered at Stage 2. She attained at Level 4, within the range expected for her Key Stage.
- *Charlie* has moderate hearing loss, which occasionally leads to lack of concentration and misunderstandings. There has been peripatetic support from the LEA hearing impaired staff at Stage 3. Charlie functions at Level 5 in numbers work, but he often needs additional teacher support explaining new concepts.
- *David* has a reading age of 6, despite intensive teaching from school staff and LEA specialists. He had lengthy periods of truancy in Years 9 and 10 but came to school regularly in Year 11. He had an IEP at Stage 3. David functions at Level 5 in numbers but requires additional teacher time to explain new concepts.
- *Edgar* had been referred to Eastville by another comprehensive following extensive bullying and truancy. He had considerable support from his form teacher, his year tutor and the home–school liaison teacher. Requests for statementing had been turned down and a note in lieu was operating. Edgar had a long history of familial abuse and delinquency. His mental arithmetic and problem solving were at or above Level 5, but he could be extremely disruptive unless the teacher was able to maintain a calm working atmosphere in the class and to resolve his anxieties about new concepts. He had an IEP at Stage 3.
- *Freddy*'s mother was a drug abuser. Despite reasonable ability, chronic truancy from primary school left him with very limited maths attainments. He needed extension material to enable him to

work at a higher level than the rest of the band on some topics. He had considerable support from the home–school liaison teacher and Education Welfare Officer at Stage 3, but despite this was delinquent and an under-age father.

- *Godfrey* had been referred to child guidance at primary school for behavioural and learning difficulties. He was thought to be an underachiever and had made good progress in the early years of secondary school, but experimentation with LSD had brought concentration, delinquency and behavioural problems to the fore. He had support from one of the special needs staff who had written an IEP at Stage 2. This included the need for extension work on some topics and help to reduce his anxieties about others.
- *Harry*'s mother had had a series of boyfriends, whom Harry resented and rebelled against. There was a pattern of delinquency and Social Services support for the family, though this was now discontinued. He truanted regularly through Years 9 and 10, but then Harry's girlfriend kept him coming to school. He had a lot of support from his teachers, but the gaps in his schooling meant that his maths remained at Level 4. Harry had an IEP at Stage 2. This included the need for structured teaching.
- *Ione* developed a passionate affair with her first boyfriend at the age of 14. She told her mother that school held nothing for her. She was a low attainer in all her subjects: in maths she was working towards Level 4. She wanted to have a baby. Child protection staff were contacted but Ione had had a good relationship with her year tutor which helped her through. She was now on the Stage 1 register, which include action plans for differentiation and extra teacher time and help on mental arithmetic from her mother.

DISCUSSION OF IEPs FOR EMOTIONAL AND BEHAVIOURAL DIFFICULTIES

The problems of the other 31 pupils in the bottom band were no less severe. Some pupils had taken overdoses, others had run away from home, others had under-age pregnancies and so forth. For all these pupils the SENCo had worked very closely with the year tutor and form teachers to coordinate learning, pastoral and counselling support within the individual education and action plans. The gathering tide of family stress, unemployment and poverty had inspired many subject teachers to develop their classroom teaching and management skills and also to spend lengthy periods of time counselling these pupils and talking through their difficulties in and out of school.

OFSTED have recently suggested that some schools offer a calm and supportive environment at the cost of not stretching their lower attaining pupils. Some schools in this particular survey would argue that this is a false dichotomy. Eastville staff would argue that it was only this degree of support which enabled so many of their less able pupils to keep coming to school and to gain exam qualifications. At the start of Year 10, seven out of the 40 had been attaining at Level 2, 26 at Level 3 and seven at Level 4 or above. By the end of Year 11, 32 of these 40 pupils were entered for GCSE maths and 28 passed.

Stage 1 identification and assessment meetings enabled the year tutor, form tutors and special needs staff to develop a coordinated strategy to ameliorate the learning, behavioural and emotional difficulties of these pupils – as well as those of average and above average ability – and to monitor trends and examine resource, staffing and training implications. Stage 1 meetings about pupils with emotional and behavioural difficulties may prove to be one of the most effective aspects of the Code of Practice, as they focus the expressions of concern among mainstream subject and pastoral staff, combine the curricular and the pastoral and offer the prospect of coordinated support involving the staff as a whole.

If half of the pupils in urban schools have temporary difficulties, requiring registration at Stage 1 at some time in their school career, a much smaller number have chronic or severe difficulties. The names of these pupils will be referred to meetings for pupils at Stage 2 or 3. Some of the SENCos in the survey felt anxious about the responsibility of deciding at what point they should be referred to outside agencies. There are no clear definitions of the thresholds between Stages 1, 2 and 3 in the Code of Practice. It is much more difficult to decide on criteria for problem behaviour than reading difficulties or physical disabilities. And there appear to be few tests or checklists available. Some LEAs are working on their own and using them as a means of generating a consensus between schools and outside agencies. Training for SENCos may well be crucial to the success of the Code in this area.

IEPs for pupils with emotional and behavioural difficulties would include references to their levels of attainment in the basic skills of oracy, literacy and numeracy as well as in the wider curriculum, their special strengths and their behavioural problems. It would be expected that all staff would be informed of the pupils' targets, through the use of, for instance, DARTs cards. This kind of target-setting can be reinforced through a coordinated staffing and INSET strategy in programmes such as Assertive Discipline, for instance.

If the problems are acute and if they persist despite the concerted, coordinated and collaborative efforts of the staff, advice or input will be sought from external agencies about the possibility of drafting an IEP at Stage 3. These agencies might include:

- child protection
- LEA behaviour support staff
- LEA learning and sensory support staff
- Education Welfare Services
- Youth and Community Services
- general practitioners
- Social Services departments
- Educational Psychologists
- clinical psychologists
- psychiatrists as appropriate.

Pupils referred to a Stage 3 meeting will have an individual learning plan as well as a behavioural management plan, incorporating the advice of the external agencies. There is a considerable difference in the use made of each of these services by schools and LEAs, but it would be unusual for more than 2 per cent of pupils to be involved with any of them at any one time.

REFLECTIONS

- How well do staff understand the referral procedures?
- Has your school drawn up IEPs for pupils with emotional and behavioural difficulties?
- How has the IEP been agreed with staff and external agencies?
- How has it been communicated?

FEEDBACK

At most of the survey schools, Education Welfare Officers, LEA behaviour support staff and Educational Psychologists attended INSET sessions and occasional Stage 1 meetings on a pre-planned basis to ensure that all staff grew familiar with the referral process. They were also brought into Stage 2 meetings to advise on school-based support. This enabled the LEA to track pupils whose behavioural difficulties were becoming extreme and to ensure that schools were doing everything appropriate to minimize the pupils' problems and to forestall exclusions. Managed as a problem-solving exercise (Moss, 1995), the drafting of a Stage 3 IEP can play its part in fostering the professional development of the staff.

CASE HISTORIES

- *Martin* was a Year 10 pupil of average ability with particular strengths in music and the creative arts. His mother had had drug problems and his father had been in prison. He himself had been disruptive in school and involved in burglaries outside. He fell one night and broke his back. During his absence, a Stage 2 individual education plan was drawn up to coordinate his GCSE course work. This also included a behavioural management plan. On his return to school, he also received extensive counselling and was 'looked after' by a group of staff and pupil 'mentors'. The level of disruption fell considerably and he was taken off the SEN register.

- *Ellie* was a Year 9 pupil of above average ability with particular strengths in technology and sport. The family had undergone periods of difficulty and change and Ellie herself was involved in drug abuse. She used her leadership qualities to foment problems in class, disrupting lessons that bored her and getting others to follow. A Stage 2 IEP was written, but she failed to respond. An LEA behavioural checklist was completed and it was clear that her difficulties were severe in terms of the LEA norms. A Stage 3 IEP was written in conjunction with the behaviour support service and the Educational Psychologist, who found her to have high scores in aspects of non-verbal intelligence. The IEP included regular input from the behaviour support service, support from a group of key staff, out-of-school sporting activities and a residential course for exceptionally talented pupils in electronics. Her mother came into the classes that she was disrupting, and worked closely with the key staff and her behavioural support teacher.

PUPIL PERSPECTIVES

Edgar, one of the pupils whose difficulties in maths were described above, had been referred to Eastville School by another school following extensive bullying and truancy. When the full extent of his problems came to light, he was fostered and left the school. He subsequently returned several times.

> 'To me, it was a little group of the teachers in my year group that made all the difference. They took me away on residentials, they kept me with them when I could not manage class work and helped me stay quiet.'

The crucial factor for Danny, another pupil in that maths group who had also been transferred from another school, was that he was able to form positive relationships with a key group of the Eastville staff – including his year tutor, form tutor, the IT teacher, members of the special needs team and the headteacher – as well as the LEA behaviour support staff.

'I've had lots of times when I was on the verge of expulsion, cheeking teachers for no reason or fighting. If I don't get any support, it makes me dead stressed out and dead tense. When I got expelled from my last school, it all started when I thought I'd done a good piece of work. I'd tried really hard. The teacher put me down. I don't know if he meant to but he did. And there was nobody to calm me down.'

Since moving to Eastville, the support of this collaborative group had seen him through a number of problems.

'There have been times when I have just been about to blow my top. Someone was always there to calm me down. [One teacher] put me in isolation with her and that helped. [Another] let me work on the computers. [The head] talks me out of it. She gets me in her office and starts talking to me. Her tone of voice is nice and she knows the things to say to calm me down.'

Networking not only helps staff to share the load; it furthers the skills of the individual staff. 'Here there's lots of teachers who care, but where I was [in my previous school] I felt I was on my own.'

SUMMARY

Since the mid- to late 1980s, there has been a considerable increase in childhood poverty and family stress. This appears to have had a serious effect on the emotional and behavioural difficulties of pupils, especially those from areas of deprivation and high unemployment. Exclusions and the demand for statements have risen. Following the Elton Report, many schools developed their own behavioural codes and policies, pursued greater consistency and explored a wider range of corporate management and support strategies. Elton referred to a 'continuum' of behavioural difficulties from the most short-term and trivial to the most severe and chronic, and in some schools these have all come to be accepted as whole-school issues.

The SEN Code of Practice has accepted this notion of a 'continuum'. Its authors argued that pupils with these problems 'fail to meet expectations in school' – and should therefore be seen as having difficulties in learning. This has led a growing number of schools to review their behavioural policies in the light of the SEN Code and to incorporate identification, assessment and individual educational plans for pupils with these difficulties into their staged special needs assessment procedures.

In these schools, SEN procedures now reflect the particular values of the whole school. All the survey schools were exercised by the growing number of adolescent overdoses, for instance, but this appeared to hold a special horror for one of the Church schools. The degree of difference could be exaggerated, however. Among the survey schools there was considerable overlap, both between the sets of rules and the rationale for placing pupils on each stage of the assessment procedure.

Some LEAs are making the use of staged assessment procedures a necessary precondition of their involvement with difficult children. They hope to use the SEN Code to resolve their two main concerns: the rise in exclusions, and equity in the use of statementing. Since the advent of local management, LEAs no longer have the power to impose their own disciplinary guidelines. Devolved management has created problems for them in the definition of the thresholds between the various stages of assessment, too. IEPs for these pupils will now act as the interface between the values of the school and those of the LEA. It is much more difficult to define problem behaviour than reading or physical disabilities and much will now depend on the ability of LEAs to generate a consensus between the schools and the outside agencies. Some are developing their own behavioural checklists as a means of underpinning this consensus. Training for SENCos and the development of their negotiating skills may be crucial to the success of the Code in this area.

It may appear to teachers that their work with these pupils is becoming progressively more demanding. Recent surveys suggest, however, that schools can and do make a difference and that their role in moral and pastoral education is respected by many young people. A coordinated staffing and inservice strategy can harness teachers' concerns, increase staff expertise and help share the load. It can also determine whether some individuals with behavioural or emotional difficulties raise their educational expectations or even survive in mainstream schools.

8

Attendance

INTRODUCTION

Before the Code of Practice was published, it might have seemed unusual to include a discussion of attendance in a book on special provision. Attendance and truancy were barely discussed by the Warnock Committee (DES, 1978, 8.89). There are no references to attendance in the chapter on the Code on school-based assessment. However, attendance is mentioned in the Code in chapter 3 on the statementing of pupils with emotional and behavioural difficulties. This argues that the LEA should seek evidence about the child's attainments, and about 'whether the child attends school irregularly' (3.68).

This is consistent with recent government policies on attendance (DfE, 1994b). The government had become noticeably more concerned about the extent and effects of truancy during the late 1980s. Circular 8/94 on *Pupil Behaviour and Discipline* includes paragraphs on truancy. Continuity of learning was also seen to be of crucial importance to the National Curriculum Council. For the SENCos in the survey schools, it had become increasingly clear that irregular attenders had particular needs which could be effectively identified and assessed within the framework of the Code.

Non-attendance affects all pupils' learning, but the problem can be especially marked for older pupils in areas of high deprivation (O'Keefe, 1994). Absence from school in Years 10 and 11 affects exam grades at all levels of ability. For low attainers, however, it can make the difference between achieving some qualifications or none at all, or between going on to further education or dropping out before the age of 16.

Responsibility for attendance will be delegated to the home-school liaison teacher, to the secondary pastoral team or the team leaders in primaries. In some schools, there is close collaboration between these staff and the SENCo (Bell, 1988). Many LEAs are adopting a five- or six-point staged approach to the identification and support of pupils with attendance problems, which mirrors that of the SEN Code and which should facilitate this collaboration.

This chapter will argue that if attendance problems could be seen as grounds for statementing, they could also be interpreted as an issue for the other stages in the SEN assessment procedure. Effective strategies for promoting good attendance and minimizing absence could play a part in the prevention of learning difficulties, and thus be seen as one more aspect of the hypothetical Stage Zero of the SEN Code. Monitoring those with irregular attendance could be seen as an aspect of Stage 1. And school-based support for pupils with acute or chronic absence problems could be seen as an aspect of Stage 2 – or 3 – whatever outside agencies are also involved. Pupils with poor attendance can benefit from coordinated action planning and IEPs.

OBJECTIVES

This chapter will include:

- reviewing whole-school policies for promoting good attendance
- exploring strategies for minimizing irregular attendance
- developing ways of preventing post-registration truancy
- reviewing ways of overcoming condoned absences
- exploring ways of supporting pupils with particular needs, caused by acute or chronic absence problems, including:

  - long-term truants
  - school phobic pupils
  - sick pupils
  - travelling children
  - pregnant schoolgirls.

DISCUSSION OF WHOLE-SCHOOL ATTENDANCE POLICIES

A number of studies have examined the relationship between child health, deprivation and unemployment on the one hand and educational attainments and attendance on the other (e.g. Fraser, 1984; Power *et al.*, 1991). In a study for Barnardo's, Wilkinson (1994) argued that

> There has been a three-fold increase in children living below the EC relative income poverty line during the 1980's. Such children make up almost a third of the average classroom. ... There is evidence to suggest that health and educational performance are affected by relative deprivation.

Wilkinson would argue that deprived families are more susceptible to colds and minor respiratory infections, as well as more serious health problems. Nevertheless, as a number of LEA studies have shown, a whole-school attendance policy, rooted in effective classroom management procedures, can do a great deal to mitigate these psycho-social pressures. Schools which involve the whole staff in identifying absence patterns and which ensure that all teachers have clearly defined roles can make a quantifiable difference, even in areas of high deprivation (Brown, 1983).

REFLECTIONS

- Is there an attendance policy in your school?
- Does this include an evaluation of absence patterns?
- In your school, how many staff check attendance every lesson?
- Who checks that daily attendance registers are kept up to date?
- How far has your school moved towards computerized registration?
- How much office time is given over to weekly attendance checks?
- How often are pupils and staff informed of attendance figures?
- How does your school use rewards to reinforce good attendance?
- How does your school use community links to reinforce good attendance?

FEEDBACK

As part of their brief in preventing learning difficulties, two of the SENCos featured in the survey carried out longitudinal surveys of attendance and found close correlations between learning difficulties in Year 7, terminal GCSE pass rates and attendance in Year 11. At Eastville in 1987, 35 per cent of pupils were leaving school with no GCSE qualifications, and attendance rates for Year 11 at Christmas were 68 per cent. Most, though by no means all, of the pupils who were leaving without qualifications had had a history of learning difficulties in Year 7. At Northville, an inner city school which had seen a striking change in employment, income and family patterns between 1985 and 1994, 32 per cent left school in 1994 with no GCSE passes, and attendance rates for Year 11 at Christmas in 1994 were 70 per cent.

The SENCos clearly saw this kind of evaluation as an important part of a hypothetical Stage Zero in the identification of the causes of learning difficulties. Once they had outlined the problem, groups of staff could be informed and begin to act. A planning meeting between head and SENCo resulted in close collaboration between senior management and pastoral teams and the office staff at East-ville. This ensured that every form teacher was told about his or her form's attendance rates every week. Registers for the previous week were closed on Monday and interim attendance scores for every form were relayed to the staff on the Tuesday morning. The names of the forms with the highest rates in each year were also posted on one of the main school notice-boards. Rewards were offered to the forms in each year with the highest group scores, or to those with the greatest improvements, two or three times a term.

What Eastville hoped to achieve by this was an increase in peer pressure by whole classes on poorly attending class members, backed up by the form tutors' encouragement. When Eastville started this attendance drive they were still using manual registers, and checking these was extremely time consuming. Before com-puterization, it could take an hour a week for pastoral staff to check the registers and another hour for the office staff to print the results, but the effects were striking and immediate. Attendance rates in Years 7–9 rose most quickly. Next to change were the numbers of hard core truants, with attendance rates of 70 per cent or less. Eventually, occasional absence among Years 10 and 11 also fell. Attendance at the Christmas mock exams rose from 68 per cent to 95 per cent and 91 per cent left with five or more GCSE passes in 1994.

At Eastville, where there was a high correlation between pupils with poor attendance records and those with learning, emotional and behavioural difficulties the problem was originally conceived as an issue for collaboration between the special needs and pastoral teams. Both contributed their own policy suggestions. The pastoral managers created their own attendance boards in their own areas, very much along the lines of Japanese car factory managers. They encouraged form tutors in their turn to phone their pupils' homes if they did not come into registration on time. Computerization en-abled letters for any lengthy unauthorized absences. Gradually, an increasing number of form tutors were drawn into policy develop-ment. They moved from simple absence checks to taking a formal register each lesson and devising their own strategies for rewarding individuals in their classes.

Urban schools like Eastville and Northville, which were part of a Compact scheme with local employers, could bring other pressures to bear. The scheme encouraged subject staff to check the attendance of all Year 10 and 11 pupils every lesson and absence would be followed up by both a form tutor and a Compact mentor. Individual Year 10 and 11 pupils with high attendance scores would be en-couraged to apply for bursary help at college or employment oppor-tunities funded by the Compact. Even with high local deprivation, the proportion of pupils gaining five or more GCSE passes soon climbed well above the national average.

DISCUSSION OF IRREGULAR ATTENDANCE

In any single school, the exact relationships between irregular attendance and family deprivation are complex and elusive. The SENCos at Eastville and Northville regularly checked the lists of absent pupils against the lists of children on free school meals and those with learning difficulties. Utilizing their LEA's research and intelligence mainframe computer, they only found a correlation of 0.35 or less, however. While there are clear psycho-social trends operating at a school level, the correlation appears to break down at the level of individual children. Some of the pupils with the greatest problems outside school rarely miss a day, whereas some of the more able or affluent pupils in urban areas have relatively serious absence problems. One year, girls will have more time off, the next it will be boys, and so on.

Evaluating large-scale absence trends and ensuring that the staff are gradually encouraged to accept greater responsibility for them can be time consuming, and even discouraging in the short term. However, a systematic approach to the prevention of absence problems can mitigate the effects of local social deprivation and help forestall a long-term cycle of impoverished family life, reduced educational qualifications and lowered employment possibilities for the next generation.

REFLECTIONS

- Who decides who is to contact the parents in your school?
- What responsibility does the form tutor have in initiating contact with parents?
- What responsibility does the pastoral manager have?
- What responsibility do the senior managers have?
- At what point are Education Social Workers contacted?

FEEDBACK

In schools where the identification and assessment of attendance problems is staged:

- Stage 1 will often be for the form tutor or class teacher to share their concern with irregular attenders and their parents and to make a record of those concerns

- Stage 2 may entail an individual education plan with targets to monitor and reinforce regular attendance
- Stage 3 can be reserved for pupils whose attendance rates cause concern to an Education Social Worker, which may result in a home visit or the first formal warning letter
- Stage 4 can be reserved for pupils with particular needs – sick pupils, pregnant female pupils, those with medical needs or those being reintegrated after long absence who need a more detailed plan
- Stage 5 for statemented pupils and those facing court appearances.

DISCUSSION OF SPECIAL PROVISION FOR CHRONIC NON-ATTENDERS

Returning to full-time education after lengthy periods of absence can be a stressful experience, even for those pupils with no complicating learning, medical or emotional difficulties. The original insistence of the National Curriculum Council that virtually all pupils had to follow all ten subjects of the National Curriculum within the levels prescribed for pupils at their Key Stage may even have exacerbated the problems of some of these pupils. The Dearing Report (1993) has allowed for a measure of flexibility and some schools in the survey made some imaginative attempts to reintegrate chronic non-attenders by utilizing individual education plans.

REFLECTION

- What has your school done to encourage long-term non-attenders to return?

FEEDBACK

Eastville and Northville offered some long-term non-attenders a 'safe haven', a small special class with extra adult support. Southville had a resource base where staff worked with pupils with individual needs. This could enable pupils who have fallen behind with their work, or who have gaps in their basic skills, to receive concentrated help. Safe havens can also function as a 'half-way house' to allow their Education Social Worker to bring them into school and pay discreet visits to carry on their support. After a brief resettling period, pupils can be encouraged to rejoin the lessons they feel most positive about and this can lead to gradual reintegration.

DISCUSSION OF LENGTHY MEDICAL ABSENCE

In the past some pupils with long-term illnesses or broken bones may have been hesitant about returning to school, particularly if there had been little contact between home, hospital and school during either the illness or the convalescence. This can become a serious issue in schools which have problems with disabled access or which continue to expect such pupils to work in isolated ground floor offices.

Some convalescent pupils with significant medical problems can be encouraged by their consultants to come back to school before the LEA has completed a statement. It may be thought that a return to school will in itself speed the therapeutic process. Careful advance planning, the involvement of peer mentors and *ad hoc* groups of staff well known to the convalescent pupil and some lateral thinking can alleviate many of these problems.

REFLECTION

- What has your school done to encourage pupils with lengthy medical absences to return?

FEEDBACK

Circular 12/94 (DfE, 1994b) on the education of sick children suggests that one member of staff acts as a 'named contact' for hospital teachers and home tutors. At Eastville this was the Special Needs Coordinator – even where the pupil had no learning difficulties in the Warnock sense. In Northville it was a pastoral manager. The Circular envisages that the 'named contact', the hospital teachers and home tutors exchange visits. Some hospitals and rehabilitation centres already encourage teachers to visit them and nurses are often happy to join planning meetings in school. Other exchange teaching materials by fax. This can be most helpful, especially in the case of GCSE course work. It is not always practicable for sick pupils to follow all ten subjects of the National Curriculum. However, poor communication between home tutors and the school can lead to an undue emphasis on routine exercises, particularly in the core subjects, and close collaboration can ensure a more engaging programme of study.

Martin, an Eastville pupil who was absent for over six months after breaking his back, undertook work in English, maths, science, history and modern languages while convalescing. He had had no learning difficulties within the Warnock definition, but he would have fallen behind with his GCSEs had he not kept up with these courses in hospital and at home. At one point, communication between the home tutor and his teachers became rather strained and his mother helped to set up a special meeting between the named contact and the home tutor.

For some adolescents, the attitudes of peers may be a crucial factor in successful reintegration (see Nolan, 1987). Where pupils are admitted to hospital on a long-term basis, they not only lose some of their confidence, they also miss out on the development of their friendship groups. Martin's mother was very anxious about the long-term effects of him not seeing his friends, and the school agreed for visits to be made by peer mentors in the weeks before his return. Some Canadian special needs teachers and parents prepare for reintegration by bringing a 'circle' of special friends together as part of the planning stage (see Gold, 1994).

DISCUSSION OF PUPILS WITH ASSOCIATED EMOTIONAL DIFFICULTIES

The return to school of pupils with emotional difficulties, such as depression, panic attacks or school phobia, may need even more careful handling, including professional advice and support from external agencies in extreme cases. It can be helpful for the named contact to attend planning meetings to look at specific issues.

Some phobic pupils with difficulties about leaving the family home may be helped by the provision of special transport. Depressed or very anxious pupils may appreciate their support worker coming into school and working with them in a 'safe haven' on a regular basis. Expensive though this may be to the external agencies, it may prove more cost-effective, as well as more helpful in the long term.

REFLECTION

- How has your school worked with external agencies to reintegrate long-term absentees with serious emotional difficulties?

FEEDBACK

Westville School has a special 'safe haven' for phobic pupils. Each time one is referred, there is a conference between the pupil, parents, the class teacher, the appropriate pastoral manager and the outside agencies. In Fay's case, these included her home tutor, her Education

Social Worker, her psychiatrist and a community psychiatric nurse. Fay had become extremely anxious about the time when her mother had been diagnosed with cancer, though there were also other longer-term child protection factors. Fay was reluctant to leave her mother, but once she had been persuaded to make the journey to school, she became calmer.

During the first week, Fay's home tutor brought her to school and stayed most of the day. Fay attended mainstream lessons but her tutor noticed that she would get particularly anxious around lunch-time. During the following week the tutor brought her to school and stayed for lunch. Thereafter special transport was arranged and Fay attended regularly for the rest of the term.

DISCUSSION OF THE INTEGRATION OF PREGNANT FEMALE PUPILS

Schools vary widely in the degree of support they give to pregnant female pupils. Some encourage them to work from home as soon as the pregnancy becomes known, others enable them to stay on for as long as they wish, sometimes well after the twenty-eighth week. The vast majority of these pupils do not fall within the Warnock definition of special educational needs and in most schools they remain the responsibility of the pastoral management. In some schools, however, the named contact is the SENCo.

REFLECTIONS

- What is your school's attitude to schoolgirl pregnancy?
- Who coordinates their educational provision?

FEEDBACK

At Southville, there were full discussions between the girls, their parents, the home and hospital service and the pastoral deputy about how long the girls wished to continue in school and what alternative provision might be required. Edwina was one of the more able pupils in her year. The pastoral deputy was so concerned about her academic potential that she used to take work round to her house and give her individual coaching.

Westville was able to use its 'safe haven'. Diane had two pregnancies before she reached the age of 15. She was looked after by Social Services. Her social worker, parents and foster-parents supported her wish to stay on at school for as long as possible. She concentrated on a narrow range of subjects, including English, maths, art and child care. For these subjects she attended mainstream classes and spent most of the rest of the week in the school's resource centre. After a time, she complained of intrusive remarks from other pupils. The issue was taken up with these pupils as an equal opportunities issue, but Diane decided to transfer to the local further education college, which also served as an LEA base for pregnant schoolgirls.

By the time Diane returned to school, the foster placement had broken down and she was staying in a Salvation Army hostel some miles from the school. The officers and her social worker supported her decision to take up part-time education at Southville, concentrating on art, child care, English language and literature. A taxi brought her to the school three days a week, the Salvation Army officers looked after the baby for the time she was at school and she eventually received four high grade GCSE passes. Her course work in English included a study of Dickens' *Hard Times* and a particularly bleak essay about peer attitudes to juvenile pregnancy.

DISCUSSION OF THE INTEGRATION OF TRAVELLING CHILDREN

Despite their equal opportunities policies, some schools have great difficulty planning provision for travelling children. Many travelling families do not have learning difficulties as defined by Warnock, though it is also true that travellers have some of the highest illiteracy rates in Europe (Jordan, 1994). There may also be problems involved in the maintenance of pupil records, and the development of suitable reading materials and distance learning texts.

REFLECTIONS

- How many travelling children have enrolled in your school?
- Could they stay in your school for a limited period and still experience continuity and progress in their education?
- Were the family involved in taking decisions about their children's education?

FEEDBACK

Eastville School was approached by the LEA equal opportunities officer who had a particular concern with travelling children to see what provision could be made for two travelling families. Josephine was 14 years old, a pupil of at least average ability but with significant gaps in her schooling. She could read and write, unlike Jane (12) and Peter (11). None of the children had been in regular attendance at school for at least two years.

After a planning meeting between the parents, pupils, SENCo and LEA officer, it was agreed that all three pupils should spend a week being assessed in the school's resource base. It was quite clear after a day or two that Josephine was capable of joining mainstream GCSE classes and she was then fully integrated. Special provision in basic literacy was arranged with the LEA learning support service for Jane and Peter and they attended Eastville every morning. They were both integrated for creative arts lessons, but it was felt that they would be unable to manage any lessons requiring reading or writing, even with special support.

Josephine's timetable was organized so that she could spend as many of her lessons as possible with staff who were supportive towards children with particular needs. In maths she picked up some topics quickly, but made slow progress in others. In English she wrote some powerful autobiographical stories, but found library research more difficult. Initially there were disciplinary problems with Josephine, especially over uniform and jewellery. The equal opportunities officers and her parents came to the school to help resolve these. The school also persuaded the mother of Jane and Peter to spend a morning in the resource base, seeing what the children were doing. Jane made some progress in basic phonics and word recognition, but Peter had more specific learning difficulties. After two terms' regular attendance, an attempt was made to burn the families out of their homes and they decided to move on, much to the chagrin of the staff who had provided them with special support. Josephine never attended school again.

PUPIL PERSPECTIVES

Attendance problems are often complex in origin. Friends and neighbours may truant. For some pupils, there may be medical problems or a history of attendance problems in the family. For others, there may be a history of learning or emotional difficulties, or there may be difficulties with specific subjects, teachers or fellow pupils. For Anita, 'It all started in Year 7. There was a teacher who picked on me. He did not like my older sister. He asked me to read in class and I couldn't read very well. I hated him.' Anita did not enjoy truanting. 'I felt guilty about nicking off. I told my mum and she went mad. She did not want me to end up like my sisters.'

Keeping a close check on registers and building closer links between parents and schools can help enormously. Anita found

'There was no one else to nick off with so I came back to school. I have been coming much more since Year 8.' Anita continued to attend irregularly but, with the support of a nucleus of staff, she took and passed eight GCSEs.

Terri, another pupil with a history of learning, behavioural and attendance problems, admitted 'I have always had the odd few days off. I nick off a bit now and again. It's mainly because I don't like lessons. It's the subjects I don't like. I like most of the teachers though.' Danny, another poor attender, agreed about the importance of the school ethos. 'If I had teachers I hated, I'd stop coming. Most of the teachers in this school are dead nice to talk to. When I was having time off in Year 9, Mrs X used to talk to me about it. My form teacher and year tutor were dead nice, too. I came in for all my GCSEs. I wouldn't have done without them.'

SUMMARY

Growing social polarization has put increased pressure on the health, educational attainments and attendance of some pupils, especially in areas of high deprivation. This can affect pupils at all points in the ability range, but it can be particularly damaging for those with a history of learning difficulties. A careful evaluation of these psycho-social trends can help raise staff consciousness and evoke real concern among a nucleus of teachers in a school. This concern can be channelled into the development of a systematic, staged approach to the identification of absentees, which can make a quantifiable difference to attendance, exam passes and staying on rates.

Regular attendance can be encouraged – at an individual, whole-class and whole-school level. Schools in local Compact schemes can also call on community support. Irregular attendance can be monitored more effectively, especially where registers are computerized and where attendance policies are well managed – with teachers and the outside agencies being given clearly defined responsibilities for specific groups of pupils.

The reintegration of long-term absentees can present particular problems for some schools, even when these pupils have no special educational needs in the Warnock sense. However, by raising staff awareness, encouraging debate about definitions of special needs and providing 'named contacts' along the lines of the 'named person', some schools have adopted rather more imaginative approaches. These have enabled mainstream staff to support pupils with learning, medical and emotional difficulties in their return to mainstream education – as well as historically marginalized groups such as pregnant pupils and travelling children.

Attendance issues can thus provide a focus for the professional development of staff and a discussion about the range of pupils whose needs can be legitimately seen as the school's responsibility. Many of the staff in the survey schools were concerned about the effects of long-term unemployment, poverty and changing family patterns on their pupils' learning, behaviour and attendance. They wanted to do something about it by nurturing a more inclusive school ethos.

9

Integrating statemented pupils

INTRODUCTION

The Code of Practice had little to say about integration. Schools have to report on 'How children with special educational needs are integrated' in their SEN policies. LEAs have to clarify and streamline their procedures for statementing. But there is no new policy initiative on the 'rights' of statemented pupils to greater integration (Barnes and Oliver, 1995). Following the Warnock Report, some LEAs transferred some groups of statemented pupils from special schools to their local schools or to special units in mainstream schools. Others, which had previously statemented relatively few children, continued to send correspondingly few to special schools. However, a few LEAs had even built new special schools. In national terms, the proportion of children being educated in special schools continued to rise after the Warnock Report was published (Swann, 1985) and recent figures suggest it has started to rise again (Vincent et al., 1995).

Even though most parents were given the right to choose their children's school in the 1986 Education Act, it was not until 1993 that this right was extended to the parents of statemented children. That is not to say that the familiar old provisos can be disregarded. Schools and LEAs do not have to comply with the parents' wishes if 'the school is unsuitable to the child's . . . special educational needs or the placement is incompatible with the efficient education of other children . . . or use of resources' (DfE, 1993b).

Government reluctance to make adequate resources available for the transfer of pupils from special schools and for the national funding of teacher retraining meant that the nationwide integration promised in the 1976 Education Act and repeatedly referred to in the Warnock Report never materialized. However, particular LEAs have achieved a great deal in collaboration with individual schools.

This is an issue which touches on a school's, a community's and a nation's fundamental beliefs about mainstream education and the pupils it should serve. Integration is not something to be imposed.

There needs to be a lengthy process of consultation – involving parents, voluntary groups, community representatives, education officials, headteachers and staff. It will not succeed unless appropriate funds are delegated, it has the headteacher's active support and the teachers are enabled to develop their skills and understanding.

Integration demands a willingness to undertake a school-wide INSET programme. A few teachers 'reach out forcefully and effectively' to these pupils (Brophy and Good, 1974). Most teachers, however, seem to appreciate an extended introduction to SEN issues, as well as ongoing courses of inservice training on topics such as identification and assessment, differentiation, the teaching of basic skills and behavioural management – sandwiched round periods of practical involvement with small groups of statemented pupils in a safe and supported environment.

OBJECTIVES

This chapter aims to:

- review the historical background
- review the use of school-based 'sandwich courses', involving small groups as a training resource in SEN provision
- review the integration of each of the groups of statemented pupils outlined in the Code, including those with:
  - learning difficulties
  - specific learning difficulties
  - emotional and behavioural difficulties
  - physical disabilities and medical conditions
  - sensory impairments
  - speech and language difficulties.

DISCUSSION OF THE HISTORICAL BACKGROUND

When the Warnock Committee discussed integration, its main emphasis was on the issue of how these children's education should be organized within existing mainstream schools, rather than on how changes to mainstream schools could be managed. It offered a staged approach to the placement of statemented pupils (DES, 1978, 7.6), suggesting that:

- some pupils would be taught full-time in mainstream classrooms

- others would have most of their education in the mainstream with short periods of small group work
- others would be based in special classes but spend a limited number of lessons in the mainstream
- others would be restricted to social integration.

One suggestion about how change might come about among mainstream teachers is outlined in this little known paragraph (DES, 1978, 7.24):

> When a special class is attached to a school, teachers in the class should have the opportunity to do some teaching in other parts of the school; conversely teachers in the ordinary classes should have the opportunity to share some of the teaching in the special class. Such interchange will promote the unity of the school.

The Committee envisaged that this kind of practical experience would be underpinned by a massive expansion of short inservice courses. It recommended that a national programme 'should be implemented without delay'. It hoped that within 'four years' of publication, i.e. by 1982, 'the majority of teachers' would have undertaken such courses. As has since become clear, the government chose not to implement this proposal.

REFLECTIONS

- Have any special schools been closed in your LEA?
- How many of the schools near yours have special units or classes?
- How many statemented pupils are integrated in your school?
- Are they integrated singly or as part of a special unit?
- How many staff have undertaken courses in the integration of statemented pupils?
- What kind of practical experience is built into such courses?

FEEDBACK

There are some groups of statemented pupils who attract more immediate concern than others, and LEAs have found it easier to harness this concern and to integrate them into the schools of their parents' choice. Most of the statemented children presently integrated into their local schools on an individual basis have sensory or physical disabilities, or borderline mild/moderate learning difficulties (Hegarty, 1993). Pupils with statements for emotional or behavioural difficulties are much more difficult to integrate (Smith and Laslett, 1993). Some are educated in mainstream schools, though these are mainly pupils who have always remained in mainstream classes. It is comparatively rare for pupils to return to the mainstream once they have attended special schools for pupils with behavioural difficulties.

An increasing number of LEAs have special units for pupils with sensory and physical disabilities and some also employ them for pupils with moderate learning difficulties, though many of these pupils function at the upper end of that ability range. These special units are often staffed with experienced and specially trained staff, who teach small groups, support pupils in mainstream classes and have a consultative role in the school. It is still unusual, though not unknown, for pupils with severe or complex learning difficulties to attend mainstream schools on a full-time basis, but the majority receive most of their education in special classes (Gulliford and Upton, 1992).

DISCUSSION OF AN 'INTERCHANGE' STRATEGY

For schools which already employ a coordinated staffing and in-service strategy for special provision for mainstream pupils, it is a small step to the 'interchange' strategy advocated by the Warnock Committee. The school timetable can be constructed in such a way that all mainstream staff have an element of special needs provision built into their work every two or three years. In one year, there might be an opportunity to carry out literacy work with mainstream pupils. In another, it might involve in-class support to statemented and non-statemented pupils in their own subject area. In a third, the teacher might be seconded to teach small groups of statemented pupils with learning difficulties on a withdrawal basis for a number of lessons (Sewell, 1988).

REFLECTIONS

- Is the support work for statemented pupils restricted to specialist staff in your school?
- Does your school offer mainstream staff the chance of working with a small group of statemented children for a few lessons?
- Do staff have this opportunity before or after they are asked to integrate these pupils into their mainstream class?

FEEDBACK

At Eastville School, where there was a special unit for 40 statemented pupils with physical disabilities, the head and SENCo had a holistic view of special provision. They drew up a five-year plan for involving the whole mainstream staff in small group work with the statemented pupils. The school was purpose-built, all on one level with a paramedical suite attached. It had a range of closed classrooms, open areas and quiet spaces for small-group withdrawal. Ten of the pupils with physical disabilities – just over a quarter – were within the ability range of the comprehensive. Just over half had moderate learning difficulties and a few had severe learning difficulties. Some also had emotional or behavioural difficulties and a few had additional sensory impairments.

Eastville adopted the staged framework for integration outlined by Warnock. Statemented pupils with significant learning difficulties who were still working towards Levels 1 and 2 in the core subjects and the humanities received most of their education on a small-group basis, but were integrated for some subjects like the creative arts. Others with moderate learning difficulties spent half of their week in small groups and half in mainstream classes. Those within the ability range expected of their Key Stage were given full-time mainstream education. Eastville's SEN policy was that some statemented pupils would be integrated all of the time and all would be some of the time. This eventually entailed a 30:50:100 per cent model of integration – based on the degree of learning needs, not the level of physical impairment.

The SEN policy was that nearly all statemented pupils were to be functionally integrated for the creative arts, vocational lessons, technology, personal and social education and on a social basis – that is, for up to 30 per cent of their timetable. The pupil numbers in the small withdrawal groups were kept low – ten full-time equivalent – and they had additional SSA support. Over the years, about three-quarters of Eastville's mainstream subject specialists had had the opportunity of teaching the small groups, but most of the teaching in any one year would be undertaken by a specialist SEN teacher. The small-group work was seen as a teacher training resource and a springboard for integration. Each year a different group of staff would be invited. All those who had had the experience of teaching one of these small groups felt extremely positive about it, and many subsequently felt confident enough to ask the SENCo for individual pupils to be integrated into their mainstream lessons.

Pupils who were at Level 2 in some subjects and working towards Level 2 in others – that is to say, pupils with moderate learning difficulties or those with complex perceptual, language and learning difficulties – were integrated up to 50 per cent of the time. These pupils were functionally integrated for the creative arts, technology and on a social basis. As soon as they attained basic literacy, they also attended mainstream lessons in English and the humanities. A few also attended science, maths or modern language lessons. Physically disabled pupils who were working at Level 3 or higher were integrated for the whole week, though they sometimes needed short bursts of in-class support from teachers or special support assistants (SSAs).

There were two trained specialist SEN teachers working with the small groups, but a proportion of these groups' timetables was taken by mainstream subject staff from every National Curriculum department. The Warnock Report suggested that it would take four years for the majority of teachers to undergo SEN training courses. Using a coordinated staffing and school-based inservice strategy, it can take five or six years. The staff development programme entails close collaboration between the SENCo and the manager responsible for timetabling. It is wisest to start with staff thought most likely to be sympathetic, confident and influential: this kind of rolling programme needs to be carefully managed.

Most of the staff at Eastville, including the head and deputies, had been given the opportunity to work with small groups of statemented pupils before they integrated them in their mainstream classes. It was felt that they would learn how to teach pupils with learning difficulties, if they started teaching the subject they felt most familiar with to a small group in a safe environment, with support from SSAs and specialist staff as required.

Some staff adapt quickly and easily to the teaching of pupils with significant learning difficulties. For the majority of teachers, this kind of work makes considerable intellectual and emotional demands. However well they know their subject, staff have to explore areas of the curriculum they are unused to teaching. They have to learn how to enable children to develop skills which most of their contemporaries take for granted. Some statemented pupils may have problems of articulation, physical movement and coordination, hearing and sight that staff may never have experienced before. The pupils may depend on electronic aids that their teachers may never have seen before, and some will exhibit emotional and behavioural difficulties which rule out conventional class management techniques. The head and SENCo at Eastville were in agreement about the staffing strategy: if staff could practise these new skills with a small group of students and generous SSA support, they would feel much more confident about working with these pupils in an integrated setting.

Such small-group work can be extraordinarily satisfying for staff who have never experienced it before. There is a strong experiential basis to the staff's learning and they are much more receptive to new ideas about teaching. Many realize for the first time that there is no simple cut-off point between statemented and non-statemented pupils. They become more sensitive to the individual learning styles of the whole range of mainstream pupils. In a coordinated staffing and inservice strategy, INSET follows the practical experience. INSET on differentiation can be much more productive if staff have previous first-hand experience of how varied children's learning can be (Vincent *et al.*, 1995). The identification and assessment of the learning difficulties of mainstream pupils also makes much more sense when staff have also learned how to teach those pupils described in the chapter of the Code of Practice about statementing:

- whose learning abilities fall well outside the normal ability range of mainstream pupils
- with specific learning difficulties
- with emotional and behavioural difficulties
- with physical disabilities or medical conditions
- with sensory impairments
- with speech and language difficulties.

DISCUSSION OF THE INTEGRATION OF PUPILS WITH LEARNING DIFFICULTIES

Among the survey schools, one of the commonest criticisms of the Code was that its original terms of reference were too tightly drawn. It abstracted the processes of identification and assessment from the everyday work of prevention and provision. In their discussions about the Code, Eastville staff expressed the view that successful integration generated a style of assessment which emphasized the positive skills and attributes of statemented pupils. The Code was more negative. It seemed to define the groups of statemented pupils by their learning deficits or disabilities – not by what they could be enabled to do with the support of mainstream staff. The fact that there was no national integration programme in the Code meant that it would be left to each separate head, governing body and SENCo to devise a separate policy, making the issue of integration appear more peripheral to everyday educational practice – and more challenging – than necessary.

The other major criticism was that the Code inferred that there were categories of special needs. The authors' reply was that they recognized that 'each child is unique' and that many of their criteria overlap. Many of the criteria used in their definition of pupils with learning difficulties are repeated in its descriptions of its other groups:

- they are not benefiting from working on programmes of study relevant to the Key Stage appropriate to their age
- they are working at levels in the core subjects significantly below that of their contemporaries
- their social or communication skills may impair learning
- there may be significant attendance problems affecting learning
- there may be significant medical problems affecting learning

As can be seen, this group covers an extremely wide range of pupils, from those with mild learning difficulties, which may be exacerbated by behavioural difficulties, such as truancy, to those with genetic disorders resulting in severe, complex or profound learning difficulties. The Code suggests that all these pupils should have individual education plans which include structured literacy and numeracy programmes and the use of IT.

This chapter would argue that there is no reason why willing and committed mainstream subject specialists should not teach these pupils, even those with severe learning difficulties. Not only do the teachers benefit from small-group work with SSA support, but the pupils themselves often achieve more when taught by mainstream subject specialists than by SEN specialists working as generalist teachers.

REFLECTIONS

- What would you see as the main advantages in integrating pupils with learning difficulties into your school?
- How would it benefit the other mainstream pupils?
- What would the main resource implications be, particularly in terms of teacher training and technology?

FEEDBACK

At Eastville, pupils with significant learning difficulties have gained enormously from the teaching of mainstream science teachers. At first these teachers were quite nervous. Only one teacher in the science department had had an initial training course in special education. Specialist SEN staff were timetabled to work alongside them for the first two years, and even after that they were given extremely generous SSA support, sometimes as many as three SSAs to ten pupils. After a while the science department undertook their own inservice training through local advisers and university courses and located support materials that were more appropriate. The statemented pupils – even those with severe learning difficulties –

really enjoyed their science lessons, and understood concepts at a higher level than had been anticipated. Some of the pupils working towards Level 1 in English and maths were capable of understanding and remembering work at Levels 2 and 3 in science.

Members of all the humanities departments also taught the special classes, and this led these mainstream subject specialists to suggest that some of these pupils could cope in mainstream classes – if only they could be placed in their own classes. Pupils with significant learning difficulties who were well within the moderate range were thus able to follow courses that led to GCSE. They felt safe with this particular teacher and enjoyed the chance to work with their mainstream peers. Having had the experience of small-group work, the teacher also knew how to adapt the course, modify materials and activities and use the appropriate IT. All the statemented pupils at Eastville followed all the subjects in the National Curriculum, including modern languages, and James, a pupil functioning at Levels 2 and 3 in most other areas of the curriculum, had a special aptitude for German. He followed this up at evening classes after he left school and passed it at GCSE.

The survey schools which integrated statemented pupils with learning difficulties reported that it enriched the work of the whole school. The mainstream pupils can also benefit. Wherever pupils with learning difficulties are integrated, they have to have extra support from subject teachers or SSAs. These pupils will often feel stigmatized if the help is focused on them alone. So the support staff are trained to support a small group of mainstream pupils, including those who have no special needs. The statemented pupils often use high technology, which then also becomes accessible to mainstream pupils. For pupils with concentration problems there always has to be a safe, calm working ethos, which also benefits other distractible mainstream pupils.

DISCUSSION OF THE INTEGRATION OF PUPILS WITH SPECIFIC LEARNING DIFFICULTIES

Most pupils with specific learning difficulties are in mainstream schools and most do not have a statement. The Code of Practice offers five main descriptors in its definition of these pupils, but many overlap with the description of pupils with general learning difficulties:

- there are extreme discrepancies between levels of attainment within or between the core curriculum subjects
- they are working at levels in the National Curriculum significantly below those indicated by their oral ability or IQ score

- they may have problems with coordination, perception, language or memory
- there may be significant behavioural problems affecting learning
- there may be significant medical problems affecting learning.

The key issue for statementing this group of pupils is the order of discrepancy between levels of attainment in literacy, spelling or maths and apparent intelligence (Pumfrey and Reason, 1991). Most psychologists would argue that there has to be a difference between reading quotient and IQ as extreme as two standard deviations before a child with specific learning difficulties can be granted a statement.

In schools which have a coordinated staffing and inservice strategy for special provision and which involve the whole staff in literacy and maths support, many of these pupils' problems can be prevented. Where small-group teaching for pupils with general reading difficulties is minimal, however, these individuals and their difficulties stand out. The school context can be decisive to the progress they make and the degree of isolation they may feel. At Eastville, the incidence of pupils with a significant difference between cognitive ability and reading age arriving as part of the Year 7 intake was 6 per cent. By the end of Year 7 this proportion had fallen to less than 1 per cent. Even in these cases, it was rare for pupils to require small-group or in-class support for more than 10 per cent of the week. There are some very unusual children with statements who require support for 50 per cent or even 70 per cent of their lessons, but most of these pupils have overlapping medical conditions. The Code suggests that pupils with statements for specific learning difficulties should have individual education plans, which include structured reading, spelling and/or numeracy programmes and the use of IT. All staff need to be alerted to the children's particular needs. Where all teachers in a school undertake training in teaching basic literacy, this can be much easier.

REFLECTIONS

- How does your school compare attainments in reading, spelling and maths with oral ability or IQ?
- What kinds of special provision are available to those with specific learning difficulties?

FEEDBACK

Pupils of average or high cognitive ability with 'dyslexia', 'dyspraxia' or even 'dyscalculia' were often referred to Eastville School. The first are pupils who have proved extremely resistant to reading and/or spelling teaching. Some arrive with virtually no reading or writing skills. Most make rapid improvements after starting a structured reading programme such as the SRA's DISTAR (Becker, 1977). This requires 10 per cent of the week of small-group work. DISTAR can be used with all pupils who have failed to learn basic phonics and it is extremely effective with about 99 per cent of the population. Some 1–2 per cent make very little progress, however.

For pupils who are resistant to DISTAR, Eastville then uses a range of multi-sensory teaching strategies. This may require up to 10 per cent of the week of individual tuition, plus another 10 per cent in small groups. Occasionally, rapid progress can follow one specific strategy, such as the use of coloured overlays, but most hard core 'dyslexics' make incremental progress each time a new approach is tried. What these pupils need is experienced reading teachers with a wealth of different strategies to offer. Failure to vary the diet, pupil truancy or other periods of absence – even the summer holidays – can start a relapse. Increasing the amount of time devoted to small-group literacy teaching beyond 20 per cent does not seem to bring much improvement.

There are other 'dyslexic' pupils who have attained basic reading skills by the end of Key Stage 2, but whose reading and spelling are well below the level of their general ability. These may be pupils who are capable of getting five A–Cs at GCSE, but a lower grade in English. Occasionally one meets pupils with university potential who can read and spell quite adequately, but not as well as one would expect. The needs of such pupils are often quite idiosyncratic. Some benefit from remedial courses such as 'Alpha to Omega' (Hornsby and Shear, 1975). Others with high analytical skills benefit from a course in etymology or the derivation of words – and this can just as easily be provided by an English teacher with an understanding of linguistics as by a specialist SEN teacher. These courses rarely require more than 10 per cent of the week in additional coaching. Most of the more able pupils with 'dyslexia' make rapid strides in as little as a term, though for a few it can be a three- or four-year slog.

'Dyspraxic' pupils may include specific learning difficulties among a range of other perceptual, coordination, linguistic or behavioural problems. Such a combination may mean that some of these statemented pupils also need speech and language therapy, occupational therapy and a careful behavioural regime. These pupils may have relatively high IQ scores and particular talents in specific areas, but will underachieve in others.

Barry was statemented because of the learning difficulties associated with his 'dyspraxia' and he can serve as an extreme example. He had particular strengths in technology and maths, but when he

:d at Eastville he could only write his name, and that only in *or* writing. He was totally illiterate. He had no idea of time, *etables* or days of the week. Though in general he was amiable enough, he could not manage in mainstream lessons without an adult at arm's length, in case he got frustrated and hit someone. Barry made rapid progress in one term using DISTAR. He learned to write using IT and gradually began to function independently. At first, Eastville felt he needed 70 per cent special class support. He started with social integration, technology and creative arts, but by the end of his third term, having reached a reading age of 8.5, he was ready for English and maths. Other 'dyspraxic' pupils have had less extreme literacy problems and no such behavioural difficulties and it was possible to initiate much faster integration programmes for them.

'Dyscalculia' is an even more unusual condition affecting the writing of numbers. At the end of Year 7, Mary was able to function in maths at Level 4 and in some strands was able to understand even more complex concepts. Her reading and spelling ages were only just below average. However, she reversed all her numbers! 102 might be written down as 501, 69 as 96. As long as she could dictate her work to a classmate or an adult she was quite successful; so the SENCo simply arranged for her to be taught in a class where a statemented pupil was already integrated, allowing Mary up to 10 per cent SSA support.

DISCUSSION OF THE INTEGRATION OF PUPILS WITH EMOTIONAL AND BEHAVIOURAL DIFFICULTIES

The last few years have seen increasing numbers of pupils with emotional and behavioural difficulties referred for statementing. More referral units have been built and more pupils excluded, the numbers tripling between 1991 and 1994 (Garner, 1994). It has proved much more difficult to generate teacher concern and to keep this group of children in mainstream schools than any other. The Code of Practice offers seven main descriptors in its definition of statemented pupils with these problems:

- a pattern of significant behavioural problems affecting learning; for example, unpredictable, bizarre, obsessive, violent or severely disruptive behaviours
- a pattern of withdrawn behaviour affecting social skills
- a history of attendance problems
- a history of eating problems
- a history of alcohol or substance abuse
- a history of bullying as either aggressor or victim
- a history of medical or mental health problems.

Because the terms of reference for the Code were drawn so tightly, there is little guidance about the prevention of such difficulties or the integration of these pupils. There is a particular problem with abstracting assessment from prevention and support, so far as this group is concerned (Smith and Laslett, 1993). It was argued by staff from some of the survey schools that staged assessment procedures could make the survival of these pupils in mainstream schools even more difficult. Staff could use the new procedures for the identification and assessment of behavioural problems to label pupils. A child who had disrupted the work of one class could be reported as 'a disruptive pupil' at a Stage 1 meeting. Staff who taught him in other classes could become more anxious about his potential for disruption. They might take more notice of his negative behaviours, thus reinforcing them. Further instances would be seen as part of a pattern and reported to a Stage 2 meeting. Persistent examples of the same behaviour could be reported to outside agencies at a Stage 3 meeting, so creating self-fulfilling prophecies (Garner, 1995; Salvia and Ysseldyke, 1985).

In its defence, it could be argued that the Code ought to be seen in the context of the Elton Report (DES, 1989) and the 1993 Circulars on the maintenance of good order in the classroom. However, most schools have drawn up clear and practical policies on discipline, attendance, child protection, health education, substance abuse and bullying. Schools which also involve the whole staff in learning support, guidance and counselling, disciplinary policy, attendance checks, health education and PSE can do much to prevent such problems overwhelming pupils.

It could also be argued that the Code of Practice encourages pastoral and special needs staff to work with each other more closely than ever before; also, under the Code, parents will have been involved as soon as problems appear. The new IEPs have to include target-setting – another way of building bridges between difficult pupils, their parents and groups of concerned staff.

In every school, there will be considerable differences between individual teachers in their attitude towards and skill in working with any given pupil. The challenge for the Coordinator will be how to help more staff to 'connect'. Teachers from two of the survey schools had devised original and effective ways of setting targets which were *D*own to earth, *A*ppropriate, *R*ealistic and *T*ime-constrained. Two schools had developed DARTs target cards for pupils, which had a picture of a dartboard on the front, a list of three agreed targets, a way of scoring each lesson and a blank timetable. The targets were to include one example of positive behaviour that the pupils knew they could deliver, promoting confidence as well as change. This call on teachers' ingenuity and empathy can go some way towards harnessing staff concerns for these individuals, enabling more staff to 'connect' and creating a more inclusive ethos in the school.

In extreme cases, some of these pupils require close individual and small-group support during periods of stress, like when they are changing schools, during a family break-up, at the death of a parent or when they represent a health and safety risk to themselves or others, if they are to be helped to remain in mainstream education. This may mean periods of reverse integration of anything between a week and two terms in a 'safe haven'. It may also mean access to a social worker or a community psychiatric nurse on a regular basis in school time, or even residential or day treatment on a psychiatric ward if necessary.

For the great majority of statemented pupils with emotional and behavioural difficulties in mainstream schools, short periods of special support in a safe haven can be followed with phased integration. There will be particular lessons that they will want to attend and specific staff with whom they feel safe. Typically the pattern of integration for these pupils is different from that of pupils with learning difficulties. Pupils with learning difficulties make almost linear progress, coping with a growing number of mainstream lessons as their confidence and basic skills increase (Hegarty, 1993). Pupils with behavioural difficulties go through a 'honeymoon' period after they have joined a new mainstream school. They feel full of energy and dislike the stigma of special class support. They want full integration immediately. Later, as some pupils' problems re-emerge, they may need periods of withdrawal and respite.

REFLECTIONS

- For how many pupils in your school has statementing been requested on the grounds of emotional or behavioural difficulties in the last year?
- How many pupils with statements for emotional and behavioural difficulties have been integrated in your school from other schools?
- How many pupils were permanently excluded in the last year and on what grounds?

FEEDBACK

In many schools, particularly those in urban areas with rapidly changing employment, income and family patterns, there is considerable concern at the increasing numbers of pupils with chronic

behavioural difficulties and the severity of these problems. Edu\
tional researchers are increasingly concerned about the pressure that
parental choice, the examination league tables and the National
Curriculum are putting on schools to exclude pupils with behavioural difficulties, particularly where these coincide with underachievement or low attainments (Garner, 1994). LEAs are concerned
about the range and flexibility of the behavioural support services
they are able to offer, the lengthening waiting lists for places in
special schools for pupils with emotional and behavioural difficulties and referral units – as well as the pressures on headteachers to
pass their pupils on to schools in areas of greater deprivation. The
police, too, are worried about the increasing numbers of difficult and
disturbed young people on the streets during school hours.

There is much that can be done to integrate pupils with this kind of
statement, provided there is a commitment from the governors, the
headteacher, the SENCo and the LEA, which can enable groups of
staff to become rather more committed, confident and effective. Katy
made her first serious suicide attempt at the age of 10. She had
recently been sent to live with her grandmother because her mother
could no longer cope with her. Shortly afterwards her dog was run
over in front of her. She picked the dog up and, though it was
covered in blood, carried the dog to the side of the road, where it
collapsed and died. Katy was terrified. She ran into the house, picked
up a bread knife and slashed her wrists. She was referred to child
psychiatry, but she later attacked her grandmother with a knife.

Katy was transferred to Eastville following a series of tantrums
and panic attacks in another comprehensive. After an initial period
of observation and coaching on her basic skills in a special class she
was reintegrated full-time. There were lengthy periods when she
could manage full-time mainstreaming. These were interspersed by
periods when her behaviour would become unpredictable, bizarre,
violent and severely disruptive. During these troubled times, she
would attend the mainstream lessons of the special group of teachers
who could cope with her: an IT teacher, with whom she had a
particularly strong relationship, the deputy head, who taught an
English class in her year, the SENCo, who taught maths to her year,
and her year tutor, who taught technology. She would spend the rest
of her lessons in a 'safe haven'. This arrangement allowed a degree of
continuity in maths and English, though even here her attainments
were well below her oral and cognitive ability. Science lessons were
more of a problem. Katy would wander around during the practical
sessions, disrupting others' work, throwing things and causing con-
frontations. She had to be excluded from science for short periods,
and provided with one-to-one teacher support during the periods of
reintegration.

Throughout her time at Eastville, Katy received support from the LEA behavioural service, Education Social Workers and the Educational Psychologist. She took nine GCSE exams – under individual supervision – and went on to college. Although there were times when her special group of staff, Katy herself, and her parents despaired, her eventual success gave them a real sense of achievement. They were conscious that were it not for the teachers' expressions of concern, Katy would have been permanently excluded long ago.

Richard was an extremely shy, withdrawn pupil, with virtually no friends at school. The family home was extremely deprived and Richard slept on the living-room sofa. He had a moderate hearing loss, he had been bullied at home, and he found it difficult to tolerate the noise of a normal classroom. He got into the habit of staying up watching videos until late, rising late and 'hanging around' on the streets. When the statementing procedure had been initiated and with the help of his Education Social Worker, he returned to school, but he would only attend regularly if he could have periods of support in Eastville's 'safe haven'. With the support of the ESW and his special group of teachers, Richard blossomed, learned to read and write, began to groom himself more carefully, look after his clothes, eat hot meals and make some friends.

Charlotte had been a long-term truant from school. She had also run away from home. When she transferred to Eastville, she was being 'looked after' by Social Services and living with a foster family. She had moments of extreme anger, self-abuse and anxiety, which were being treated by a clinical psychologist and for which a statement was initiated. She spent a lengthy period in the 'safe haven', needing differentiated work because of her particular talents. Her special team was made up of a psychologist, a mainstream English teacher whom she had met in the special class, a mainstream technology teacher who encouraged her to go on an 'outward bound' residential course and to take part in an end of term concert, an art teacher whom she met at rehearsals and the manager of the 'safe haven'. She was entered for art GCSE one year early and, after two terms' instruction, passed at Grade A.

Godfrey was given a statement in the first year of secondary school, after his first serious suicide attempt. He was failing at school and being bullied. He had night epilepsy. He had been transferred to a special school for pupils with learning and behavioural difficulties, even though his cognitive abilities were well within the range of mainstream pupils. He was then transferred to Eastville and, within a term, had made over two years' progress in his reading and learned how to write at length. There was a phased integration programme, which allowed Godfrey to return to the special class whenever he felt under pressure. His special team included the teacher from the LEA behaviour support services, who saw Godfrey two or three times a week during the most stressful periods, a psychologist and a small group of mainstream staff.

At Eastville, as in many other 'inclusive' schools, special provision entails the coordinated efforts of small groups of mainstream staff and outside agencies. Together, they can do a great deal to support statemented children at the extreme end of the continuum of behavioural difficulties. The challenge for committed SENCos is whether they can stand firm against the other more exclusive and divisive forces in schools and society.

DISCUSSION OF THE INTEGRATION OF STATEMENTED PUPILS WITH PHYSICAL DISABILITIES OR MEDICAL CONDITIONS

Many LEAs integrate statemented pupils with physical disabilities or medical conditions, either singly in their neighbourhood schools or through special units. These pupils often evoke considerable concern from mainstream staff, but it is relatively easy to harness this in order to provide coordinated provision (Hegarty, 1993). The Code of Practice offers five main descriptors in its definition of these pupils:

- there are significant discrepancies between their levels of attainment in the National Curriculum and those of their peers
- they are working at levels in the National Curriculum significantly below those indicated by their oral ability or IQ score
- they are unable to access the curriculum without close supervision and/or adaptations to materials or environment
- there may be significant self-help/safety issues
- their inability to take a full part in school activities places them under significant emotional or physical stress.

Although the Code refuses to differentiate pupils on the grounds of disability, it emphasizes individual emotional and physical stress. This need not imply that these pupils should attend special schools. A very few pupils whose conditions are deteriorating may need periods of small-group support. Pupils who have not thrived in previous mainstream schools may also need extra support until they have recovered their confidence.

For the majority, it is the level of learning difficulty that usually determines the speed and degree of integration. Pupils with extreme mobility, coordination and articulatory problems may be able to play a full part in mainstream classes, provided their cognitive ability is within the range of the mainstream pupils. Disabled pupils with moderate learning difficulties can become integrated, provided there is positive leadership from the headteacher and governors and a whole-school teacher training and support strategy. Even disabled pupils who are at Levels 1 and 2 in the core curriculum can benefit from an inclusive education.

Two decades after the Warnock Committee was set up, there are still insufficient numbers of mainstream schools that are completely accessible to pupils with mobility difficulties or that have enough trained SEN support teachers and SSAs to develop differentiated materials and activities with which to enable pupils to learn independence skills and to maintain a safe environment. Disabled researchers like Aspis (1992) and Oliver (1992) would see this as an example of 'social oppression'. The whole-scale integration of disabled pupils involves resourcing issues which can only be resolved when the political will is there.

REFLECTIONS

- How many statemented pupils with physical disabilities are there in your school?
- How much integration are they offered?
- How does your school manage the self-help and safety concerns?

FEEDBACK

Parental choice means that an increasing proportion of pupils with physical disabilities are applying for places in mainstream schools. In some cases this has led to consultation and action on improved access to the school. The LEA, Social Services, health and safety experts and voluntary groups have offered their support to schools to install lifts and ramps, widen doors and rethink fire precautions. IT provision for the whole school has to be reconsidered to allow pupils access across the curriculum and at home. SSAs are often employed to work with individual pupils or small groups and special transport is laid on.

Provided they have been given some sort of preliminary training and support, staff often show extraordinary commitment in helping these pupils to succeed in their classrooms.

Isabel could manage the stairs at home and had been fully integrated at her primary school, despite coordination and articulatory difficulties. The idea that Isabel would ever have attended a special school had not even occurred to her mother. When the deputy head of Greenville, Isabel's comprehensive, telephoned to make the initial enquiry about a transfer to Eastville, she was extremely distressed. She had been personally involved in the plans to help her to integrate and use a computer for her written work – and these had proved successful. The mother and deputy head had also enabled her to communicate with a wide range of teachers and friends. The staff had gone to extraordinary lengths to help her overcome the school's access problems. When the difficulties of moving around this two-storey, two-block school defeated Isabel, her form tutor and class had sent a present and a farewell card.

Caroline transferred to Eastville from another mainstream school, following an operation to lengthen the bones in her legs. She had also wanted to stay in Whiteville, her neighbourhood school, and the school itself was very supportive. However, the fact that Whiteville had three storeys and two blocks meant that Caroline had to move to a school with easy access. She was using a wheelchair for the first time and she was anxious that her legs were vulnerable to knocks, but she persisted with her exam lessons and took a range of GCSEs in integrated classrooms. She attracted caring support from all her teachers. She was taken to and from mainstream lessons, first by SSAs and then by her friends. She would arrive late and leave early to avoid the rush on the corridors.

Many cancer specialists now accept that a speedy return to full-time schooling can aid the recovery process, even when the children themselves may still be feeling ill and anxious. Sometimes, the parents of such children find this hard to accept and it may take months of tactful negotiation to bring this about. Gordon, who had always been in the mainstream at Eastville, missed a lot of school because of nausea and headaches. He felt less conspicuous and safer in Eastville's special unit. The consultant and nurses wanted him to make an immediate commitment to full-time integration, but in his case the school felt he had to make the decision in his own time. When he did feel ready to integrate, he had the support of all the staff. He took a number of GCSEs and passed five subjects at Grades A–C.

DISCUSSION OF THE INTEGRATION OF STATEMENTED PUPILS WITH SENSORY IMPAIRMENTS

Sensory impairments attract very similar concern from mainstream staff and the descriptors in the Code of Practice are also alike:

- there are significant discrepancies between their levels of attainment in the National Curriculum and those of their peers
- they are working at levels in the National Curriculum significantly below those indicated by their oral ability or IQ score

- there is clear recorded evidence of hearing loss or visual diffi-culty
- there is clear recorded evidence of their inability to access school life including the curriculum without adaptations
- their inability to take a full part in school activities places them under significant emotional stress.

Again, it is significant that the degree of hearing or visual impair-ment is not raised by the Code. Sensory impairment in itself need not become a bar to integration (Chapman and Stone, 1988; Webster and Wood, 1989). The important issues are special educational needs and the ability to thrive in a mainstream school, given the appropriate educational provision.

The Code suggests that all these pupils should have individual education plans, which address such matters as the child's position in class, the scope for paired support from pupils, support from specialist teachers, SSAs and technicians and the use of specialist technology, aids and equipment. For pupils with hearing impair-ment, this equipment might include appropriate hearing aids and microphones. Support staff will be specially trained and may be able to use total communication or a mixture of signing and oral speech, as appropriate (Webster and Wood, 1989).

For those with visual impairment, the equipment may include the use of handrails, lighting, voice synthesizers, enlarged or adapted worksheets, diagrams and maps or brailling machines. Support staff may need training in the use of Braille (Chapman and Stone, 1988). For pupils with sensory impairment and overlapping learning diffi-culties, there would also be a need for structured programmes in the core curriculum and small-group support for a proportion of the week.

REFLECTIONS

- How many statemented pupils with sensory impairments are there in your school?
- How much integration are they offered?
- How does your school manage the communication and safety concerns?

FEEDBACK

Parental choice means that an increasing proportion of pupils with sensory impairments are also applying for places in mainstream schools on an individual basis or as part of an integrated unit. IT provision for the whole school has to be reconsidered to allow pupils access across the curriculum and at home. Specially trained teachers and SSAs may be employed to work with individual pupils or small groups and special transport laid on.

Eastville was able to integrate pupils with complex problems which included physical disabilities, learning difficulties and hearing and visual impairment.

A brain tumour affected Clara's concentration, short-term memory, balance and sight. She lost the ability to read normal-size ink print, and had to work from enlarged worksheets. She had always been good at art and chose to start her integrated lessons there. Claire used a radio microphone in lessons, but despite her significant language and learning difficulties, she too started her integrated programme in creative arts and took art GCSE.

DISCUSSION OF THE INTEGRATION OF STATEMENTED PUPILS WITH SPEECH AND LANGUAGE DIFFICULTIES

The Code of Practice offers four main descriptors in its definition of these pupils:

- there are significant discrepancies between their levels of attainment in the National Curriculum and those of their peers
- they are working at levels in the National Curriculum significantly below those indicated by their oral ability or IQ score
- there is clear recorded evidence of difficulties in expressive or receptive language
- their inability to take a full part in school activities creates significant emotional or behavioural difficulties.

The Code again suggests that all these pupils should have individual education plans, which address such matters as the child's position in class, the scope for paired support from pupils, support from specialist teachers, SSAs and technicians and the use of specialist technology, aids and equipment (Hallahan and Kauffman, 1991).

REFLECTIONS

- How many statemented pupils with language difficulties are there in your school?
- How much integration are they offered?

FEEDBACK

Because of its speech therapy provision, Eastville integrated a number of statemented pupils with speech and language difficulties, some of whom had overlapping physical disabilities and some not.

Davinia had an unusual genetic condition which affected her articulation, the movement of her lower lip, her swallowing, her hand movements and her walking. The fact that her mother did not speak English as a first language made labial sounds especially difficult for the professionals to understand. The initial psychological assessment suggested that Davinia had moderate learning difficulties and she was sent to a special school. Her parents realized she could read maps at the age of 8 and they moved house to enable her to join an integrated Unit. Here she made rapid progress in reading. Despite therapy, her speech was still difficult to understand by the time she got to Eastville, but once she could read and use IT, she was able to join mainstream classes.

Charles did not speak until he was 4 and it was only when he had been prepared for surgery on his ears that the ENT consultant realized he was not deaf. He had complex semantic pragmatic difficulties, affecting his ability to make sense of language and to appreciate the rhythmic interplay of speech. At his parents' insistence, Charles remained in mainstream schools throughout his career, first with the support of his own special teacher and then at Eastville, through the support of a special unit. He had great difficulties with the non-verbal aspects of conversation, maintaining eye contact and standing at an appropriate distance from people. He would become either very frightened or extremely aggressive if people invaded his space.

Charles always needed very close support from a teacher or a support assistant. As he learned to read and write and express himself through art and technology, he developed other ways of acknowledging feeling and ideas. He had particular gifts in spatial mathematics and his poetry was often articulate and interesting. As his confidence in his own abilities grew, he learned a new range of conversational skills.

DISCUSSION OF SPECIAL SUPPORT ASSISTANTS

Special support assistants (SSAs) often play a crucial role in the integration of statemented pupils. For those with physical disabilities, part of that role might involve assisting with health and welfare, such as lifting children, helping them with toileting or moving equipment around the school. For those with severe sensory impairments, SSAs might need to assist with Braille or signing. It is the responsibility of teachers to provide appropriately differentiated material, but the SSA will need to adapt teaching tasks for all those with learning difficulties and help to explain it in ways the pupils will understand.

Glenys Fox (1993) would argue that SSAs need to:

- be clear about their roles and responsibilities
- understand the school's communication systems
- be seen as a positive part of the school's special needs provision
- act as part of a team
- ensure their personal interests and skills are used
- meet their needs for professional development.

REFLECTIONS

- How many SSAs work in your school?
- Do they have a job description, a timetable and a professional development plan?

FEEDBACK

With its 40-place unit for statemented pupils with physical disabilities, Eastville employed six special support assistants. When an audit of their work was carried out, it was found that 15 per cent of their time was spent on health and welfare tasks, such as lifting, assisting with rebound therapy (trampoline work) and hydrotherapy, 10 per cent on preparing differentiated materials for teachers, 35 per cent on supporting pupils in mainstream lessons and 35 per cent in small-group work, for example, teaching pupils to read. The SSAs had a job description, which they helped to devise and were time-tabled to work with specific pupils and groups through the week.

SSAs had their own weekly meetings with the paramedical staff and special needs manager. They also attended a special needs forward planning forum with senior managers from the schol, LEA officers and health trust managers once a term. They attended annual pupil review meetings and played a full part in loading pupil reports on to a computer. They had access to the school calendar, and to the weekly diary. They helped to plan their own timetables and worked together as a team in creative arts lessons, in withdrawal groups and in the hydrotherapy pool. The SSAs had had initial NNEB training as well as school-based training in IT, computing, the National Curriculum and the core skills which underpin it. Some had also undertaken courses in teaching literacy or rebound therapy.

When the special needs unit first opened, some of the teaching staff were unaware of what the pupils were capable of or the role of the SSAs. Teaching staff would tell the SENCo that they would be happy to receive SSA support, but then tell the support assistants that their help was not needed. As more of the teaching staff began to work with small groups of pupils with significant learning difficulties, they began to appreciate help, setting clear targets for the SSAs which linked into pupils' attainment targets and growing independence skills. Teachers and SSAs would work as more of a team, negotiating adaptations to teaching materials. The staff grew more sensitive to the SSAs' needs, helping them as they learned classroom management skills. It took the SSAs time to assert themselves with older mainstream pupils – especially those with more extreme behavioural difficulties. At first the pupils would defy them, saying 'You're not a teacher!' The SSAs learned to respond with a quiet but firm 'Pardon?', reminding the pupils of the rule that every adult had the right to pupil respect in that school.

PUPIL PERSPECTIVES

For some pupils, the process of leaving a mainstream school and going to a special school or unit can be traumatic. As Isabel recalled,

'My life went well until I was 11. I never really had to think of myself as handicapped at junior school. I had always joined in everything. There had been occasions when I'd felt different, but these were occasions, not a way of life. I'd really looked forward to Greenville. Unfortunately it wasn't planned for handicapped pupils and the access was bad. I loved my new school and my teachers, and loved being with my friends. But as the days and weeks went by, I grew more and more tired. With my tiredness, my disability began to show to others – though at the time not to myself. Eventually I couldn't walk or talk and my mum insisted I came to Eastville.

'Leaving Greenville and coming to Eastville was the worst day of my life. I hated my mother and I hated my teachers and most of all I hated Eastville. I had always seen myself as the same as everyone else. I had fought to be the equal of my friends. I'd tried so hard, yet they all decided I was fit for nothing other than a special unit. I had got so exhausted, I had to go to hospital for a fortnight.

'I started Eastville determined not to like it. The trouble was – it wasn't too bad. It had a heated pool and the physio let me go in every day for a fortnight. I gained a lot from her. She talked to me and let me talk to her. With so many other handicapped pupils in the school, I was reminded of my own handicap every day. No one else saw that as a problem for me. At first I felt I did not want to be judged, yet I did a lot of judging. I felt I had to mix with people I did not want to be associated with. I was scared of other people seeing me, the way I was seeing handicapped people. I felt labelled.

'I couldn't have coped at my old school. It was old-fashioned and wasn't even that well planned for physically able kids. Being at an integrated school has been hard work. It's been a struggle all the time, but it's also been beneficial, both physically and mentally. It's made me look at myself. I'm not always good at coping with situations, but I know there are always people I can talk to. I've learned a lot – about myself and other people – and I'm still learning. But I still get angry at the thought that I couldn't go to school with my friends.'

SUMMARY

Some commentators would argue that the Code, with all its emphasis on 'thresholds' and 'triggers', could yet lead to the exclusion of more pupils with learning, physical, sensory or behavioural difficulties from mainstream schools. The 1993 Education Act, from which the Code originally derived, certainly reiterated that integration should be conditional on all the old provisos – the 'suitability of the school', the 'efficient education' of other children and the efficient 'use of resources'. The Act introduced the notion that the parents of statemented pupils had the right to choose their schools, however, and it may be that this will have a more positive long-term effect on integration than the Warnock Report.

LEAs have often found it easier to integrate pupils with physical or sensory difficulties, or those at the upper ability range of moderate learning difficulties, either singly or through special units. There *are* examples of statemented pupils with severe or complex learning difficulties in mainstream classes – but these are much less common. Teachers will often show considerable concern for integrating pupils. Successful integration seems to depend on:

- appropriate funding
- full consultation between the LEA, parents, governors and the community
- the positive commitment of the head
- a coordinated staffing and professional development strategy
- the effective management by the class teacher of any additional support
- effective communications within school and between home and school.

Schools which have already adopted a coordinated staffing and inservice model for special provision for non-statemented pupils can use this as a means of managing the integration of statemented pupils. *Ad hoc* groups of mainstream staff can be invited to teach pupils with learning difficulties in small groups or through in-class support. The experience of teaching in a safe, secure environment can be beneficial to staff and pupils. Inservice work on identification and assessment, or other SEN issues like teaching basic skills or differentiation, can then follow the practical experience. At first the most sympathetic and influential staff can be involved, but the experience can gradually be extended to the staff as a whole.

At present the greatest problems lie in the integration of pupils with emotional or behavioural difficulties. Changing patterns of employment, income and family life are putting more pressure on some pupils. Competition between schools to attract high attainers seems to have led to increased exclusion rates and more requests for statementing. Such a combination of stresses can make it more difficult to evoke, harness and coordinate staff concern. As a recent LEA report concluded, while provision for most statemented pupils in mainstream schools is often of 'high quality ... support for those with challenging behaviour is inadequate'.

One starting point for the headteacher, the SENCo and concerned colleagues may be a programme of inservice work designed to increase staff confidence and assertiveness in managing challenging behaviour in general. The use of individual education plans with challenging pupils may enable pastoral staff, SENCos and senior managers to work more closely together. They may be able to generate greater commitment and ingenuity and more careful targeting of positive behaviour. And it may be that groups of teachers who are known to relate particularly well to individuals with behavioural difficulties and who are named in their IEPs as their support staff can act as role models for a wider circle of colleagues.

For some disabled writers, the failure to afford integration should be seen as 'oppression' (Aspis, 1992: Barnes and Oliver, 1995). For some pupils, removal from one's friends and local community can be 'the worst day of my life'.

10

Conclusion

RECENT TRENDS IN THE DEFINITION AND RESOURCING OF
SPECIAL PROVISION

The opening chapter of the Warnock Report gives an optimistic and
largely uncritical account of the development of special education
(Tomlinson, 1982). The Committee argued that there had been gradual progress from 'individual and charitable enterprise' to government efforts to 'support voluntary effort' and the eventual creation
of 'a national framework'. Warnock predicted that this framework
would soon incorporate 'improved provision in ordinary schools'
for the pupils who had previously been receiving remedial education, as well as for those who were to be integrated from special
schools.

As the last few years have demonstrated, however, historical
trends are rarely unambiguous. The publication of the Warnock
Report was followed by a rise in the proportion of pupils in segre-
gated special schools (Swann, 1985). The effects of subsequent government reforms like league tables of exam results and greater
parental choice – for all except statemented pupils – were to further
isolate and marginalize pupils with special needs. The proportion of
pupils in special schools has recently begun to rise once again
(Vincent et al., 1995), as have the requests from schools for formal
assessments (Lunt et al., 1994) and the numbers of excluded pupils
(ACE, 1992). There have been concerns about deteriorating standards in reading among low attainers in areas of high deprivation
(Lake, 1991; Francis and Turkington, 1992). And despite the overall
improvement in GCSE scores, especially among the most able, there
has been a marginal fall in the GCSE pass rates of the lowest 15 per
cent (Hugill, 1995).

Local management of schools and the growth of the grant maintained sector undoubtedly reduced the possibility of a national
framework for mainstream special provision. Competition between
schools has led some to adopt more 'exclusive' pupil recruitment
policies. Eager to employ more subject specialists for the National

Curriculum, some headteachers slimmed down their special needs staffing. As Professor Sally Brown (1994) put it, 'These innovations were not introduced first and foremost for children with special educational needs, and predictions for comparable innovations' effects on education in England are gloomy'.

> Several commentators ... have suggested that the combined effects of the National Curriculum and LMS may have adverse effects for pupils with special educational needs. The pressures on schools to deliver the curriculum, to produce good results, to manage their budgets and set their own priorities have led some schools to become rather less willing to support pupils with SEN.
>
> (Evans and Lunt, 1994)

There were no national surveys of the redistribution of resources away from mainstream special provision in the late 1980s, but even among the survey schools, which had been chosen as examples of SEN good practice, there were signs of reductions in resourcing. It was also clear that some secondary special needs departments in the locality had been cut from three staff to two. Some primaries had seen a long-term reduction in SEN staffing and had only been able to compensate through increased voluntary help. Some SENCos, who had been working in areas of increasingly high social deprivation and who had developed some bold and innovative work with pupils with special needs, had had to survive on stationary budgets. Other schools, which had suffered a slight overall drop in pupil numbers over the years but which had seen a rise in the absolute numbers of pupils with poor reading ages, had had to cope with reduced levels of resourcing.

These recent resourcing and policy trends have left writers like Philip Garner (1995) and Katy Simmons (1994) pessimistic about the prospects of the Code of Practice. They argue that the role of the SENCo has now become too 'onerous', given the lack of 'remuneration'. Few other staff have had the necessary training to allow them to identify or assess special needs or to provide appropriately differentiated work. As a result, they argue that mainstream staff are more likely to stereotype and label pupils, further reducing expectations and attainments. The new paperwork is too 'bureaucratic' and time consuming, and many schools are not prepared to allow pupils a voice in addressing their individual needs.

Despite all these pressures on mainstream schools and their SENCos, there have been continuing attempts to reconstruct and develop their roles, even before the Code of Practice was published. Gary Thomas and Anthony Feiler (1988) looked at team teaching, and the effect this has had in changing the 'ecology' of classrooms and schools. They argued that the needs of the individual child cannot be met in isolation; they have to be seen in a wider context. 'Planning for special needs has to be a joint exercise, involving all the ... participants.'

Through her work as a consultant to a range of inner London schools for over a decade, Gerda Hanko (1993) also emphasized the importance of team building as a way of enabling teachers of 'those who are difficult to teach' to resolve their own and the children's difficulties. She had been running INSET meetings with SENCos in lunch breaks and after school, persuading groups of staff to listen to their most troubling children and to present their individual needs in the form of case studies. She would then offer these staff a problem-solving approach, drawing up an individual plan for the pupils, giving the staff a new sense of respect and creating a mutually supportive team.

Alan Dyson (1993) has also worked for a number of years with groups of particularly 'effective' SEN Coordinators, who had attempted to reconstruct their roles and reach out to a wider range of pupils and colleagues 'through fluid, problem-solving teams'. He had found a range of practitioner/researchers who had been actively consulting their colleagues about their concerns and the kinds of support they wanted. Meg Pickup (1995), for example, argues that an important part of the SENCo's role is the development of a new SEN 'philosophy' through:

- collaborative working methods within the school
- cooperative enquiry
- collaboration and discussion with other SENCos
- an open-minded approach.

As a result, definitions of special need have grown in some schools to include those with attendance problems and underachievers across the ability range, as well as those in the original Warnock categories. There is pressure from a number of SENCos, who believe that if learning difficulties are to be prevented there should be a Stage Zero, to allow special needs concerns to influence related areas of school policy, like whole-school assessment and teaching and learning styles.

What unites so many of these writers and practitioners is a philosophical or sociopolitical stance, a set of assumptions that:

- provision for pupils with special needs cannot be left to special schools or individual SENCos
- a sizeable group of mainstream teachers share a 'concern' for the marginalized
- these teachers listen to their most challenging pupils and learn from them

- special provision should enable mainstream schools to be more 'inclusive'.

'Inclusive schools' are often sceptical about the idea that special education is to be provided by 'experts' who take their colleagues' problems away and resolve them. If SEN assessment is too 'onerous', it must be shared. If the paperwork is too 'bureaucratic', it must be streamlined. If colleagues have never 'listened' to individual pupils discussing their special needs, time must be found. These SENCos do not wait for the government to provide inservice training. They prefer a strategy which enables them to work in teams with other well-inclined subject and class teachers, who can encourage each other to reflect on their own views of special needs, and who can provide each other with the training they want on site.

The efforts of the DfE officials who framed the Code of Practice to listen to parents, teachers and voluntary groups have done a great deal to prepare the ground for a new consensus and a new confidence. Without themselves advocating a new philosophy of special provision, they emphasized the importance of openness, effective liaison and close collaboration. SENCos must work 'closely with their fellow teachers'. They have responsibilities for 'liaising with and advising fellow teachers' and 'contributing' to their inservice training. According to the Code, schools should be 'open and responsive to expressions of concern and information provided by parents'. The Code underlines the role of the 'expressions of concern' of parents, teachers and outside agencies, especially at Stage 1, where 'early identification, assessment and provision' can enable many children to 'learn and progress normally'.

IN-CLASS SUPPORT VERSUS SMALL-GROUP WORK?

The concerns of many teachers about falling reading standards, especially in the areas of high deprivation, have led practitioners, including some of those in the survey schools, to re-evaluate the relationship between small-group withdrawal work and in-class support. Both approaches have their advantages and drawbacks. The arguments are complex, but they suggest that a balance needs to be struck, and that their effectiveness depends, first, on how flexibly they can be employed, and second, on the school's general staffing policy.

Full-time withdrawal to a special class or small group, which is taught by a special needs teacher, would seem to be both ineffectual and ideologically unacceptable in 'inclusive' schools. The main disadvantages are that full-time special needs classes can lower expectations and reduce access to the 'broad, balanced curriculum'. The special needs staff simply cannot cover the whole of the National Curriculum in sufficient depth. The two main advantages of integration with in-class support are that it can enable pupils with special needs to work alongside their mainstream peers and to be taught the National Curriculum by specialist subject teachers.

The main drawback of in-class support, however, is that it can do little to teach basic skills like literacy. The advantage of short-term withdrawal work is that it can make a difference to literacy (Lingard, 1994). Short bursts of reading recovery can result in short-term gains. But, as has been clear for many years, if the children then return to the classes where they had just fallen behind, these short-term gains fade away (Collins, 1961; DES, 1975). One way of generating long-term progress in basic literacy is to employ the pupils' regular teachers as reading coaches, so that when the pupils rejoin their classes, these staff are more aware of their special needs. Having been trained in the teaching of reading, and learned greater practical understanding of special needs, these coaches can then be re-timetabled for in-class support and other special provision which can be negotiated.

The management of this kind of coordinated staffing and inservice strategy was central to the earliest definitions of the role of the Special Education Coordinator (Sewell, 1982). Alan Dyson (1993) refers to such teams and their potential for the management of change as an example of 'adhocracy'. He himself derives the term from management theorists like Henry Mintzberg (1973), Alvin Toffler (1980) and Tom Peters (Peters and Waterman, 1982) and the educationalist Thomas Skrtic (1991). These writers argue that in terms of rapid change, complex multi-layered bureaucracies, with hierarchical, clearly defined departments, were often too inflexible to cope. Modern industries, which need to manage change and respond quickly to turbulent market conditions, thrive on flexible, inter-departmental teams, brought together on an *ad hoc* basis, collaborating on specific projects, and able to take on a multiplicity of roles.

For some SEN researchers/practitioners, the either/or debate about small-group work and in-class support is best 'reframed' in terms of a staffing and INSET strategy, which takes account of wider changes in schools and the workplace. Rather than being full-time class teachers, facing a whole class lesson after lesson, teaching the same subject or the same group day in, day out, finding the same pupils failing or misbehaving again and again and passing their greatest problems on to SEN departments and the outside agencies, the teachers in an 'inclusive' school start by reconstructing their own roles. With the SEN Coordinator as 'mentor', they learn to resolve the pupils' problems by 'multi-tasking' – or juggling a 'portfolio' of different roles.

The terms 'reframing', 'portfolio' and 'mentor' are derived from the work of Charles Handy (1993), another management theorist. He saw that companies with inflexible hierarchical structures could easily lessen motivation and discourage creativity, unless staff were encouraged to vary their work over time. 'Multi-tasking' and 'juggling' have also been adopted by feminist management theorists to describe the 'workplace revolution' (Cooper, C., 1993), through which more and more women have learned to alternate the demands of a career and family.

In addition to their work as mainstream subject or class teachers, staff who take part in a coordinated SEN staffing and training strategy are encouraged to negotiate a variety of discretionary part-time roles, teaching a small group to read for one term, providing in-class support for statemented pupils the next, generating appropriately differentiated materials for more able and talented pupils for the third term, and so on. For students and newly qualified teachers, a small amount of time set aside for special needs provision at the start of a teaching career can provide valuable insights, based on first-hand experience. For those returning to teaching after a career break, it can provide an opportunity to reflect and reorientate. For settled staff who share a sympathetic concern for the growing numbers of the marginalized, it can provide a welcome and hopefully creative variety.

In this scenario, the role of the SEN Coordinator will be closer to that of a school-based 'project manager' than that of a head of department or teacher with subject responsibility. First and foremost, he or she will be managing a staffing and training strategy, whose aim is to get the most out of the available staff and whose objectives are:

- to form and re-form teams of well-intentioned colleagues
- to help them to learn how to pass on basic skills in literacy, oracy and numeracy
- to enable them to support one another and one another's pupils in their classrooms across the curriculum
- to enable them to develop appropriately differentiated materials and activities for pupils at both extremes of the ability range
- to work more effectively with difficult and disturbed children
- to help them learn how to integrate statemented pupils
- to share the responsibilty for SEN identification and assessment.

Coordinated SEN staffing strategies, underpinned by shared policies and stimulating inservice programmes, can provide a focus for schools' creativity and their most cherished values. For too long, governments have blamed schools for failing pupils with special needs, while they themselves have not willed the resources needed to retrain the profession (Mittler, 1994). Coordinated special provision, based on the collaboration of well-inclined mainstream teachers, appeals to teachers' hearts and heads.

THE CONTEXT OF EDUCATIONAL UNDERACHIEVEMENT AMONG THE LESS ABLE

Coordinated special provision draws on the concern, manifested by many mainstream staff – such as those interviewed in the research project on the moderation of SEN registers – for marginalized pupils. Teachers in urban and inner city areas, particularly, are aware of a growing underclass of poorer families (Bradshaw, 1990) with few educational qualifications, and difficulties in the basic skills. Until the 1970s, the gap between the richest and the poorest was narrowing (Townsend, 1991). As the post-war economy grew, everyone became more affluent. Remedial and special needs provision was targeted at schools with the largest numbers of pupils in receipt of free school meals. It was in effect another way of narrowing differentials between the children of the rich and poor. There was an optimistic assumption that special needs provision would remediate basic skill deficits, particularly in reading, and thus enable the least able pupils to retain access to employment opportunities.

Unfortunately, remedial education did not prove very effective in either educational or economic terms (Sewell, 1982; Bines, 1986). It perpetuated low expectations, it rationalized 'sink classes' with narrow curricular aims and poor pre-vocational preparation and it allowed many children to leave school semi-literate. It also played its part in ensuring that competitor economies, like those of Japan and Germany – which had higher expectations of their less able pupils – were able to create a wider skills base for their workforces and thus take greater advantages of structural economic shifts and technological changes.

In the mid-1980s, however, partly as a result of these structural changes and partly as a result of government policy, the gap between the rich and poor in Britain had begun to widen. Poorer families had not only fallen behind in relative terms; according to many researchers; they were worse off in absolute terms. Parents may have become unemployed, some of them on a long-term basis, or if they had a job, it may have been part time, poorly paid or insecure:

> During the 1980s children bore the brunt of changes which occurred in economic conditions, demographic structure and social policies in the UK. More children were living in low income families, and financial poverty doubled. Inequalities also became more widespread.
>
> (Bradshaw, 1990, p. 42)

At the same time as employment patterns began to change, so did family structures – at all levels in society. This combination of rising poverty and the changes in family structures exacerbated the psycho-social problems of some children and young people (Rutter, 1995). There has been a worrying increase in eating disorders, particularly among girls. Boys had always outnumbered girls in terms of literacy, learning and behavioural difficulties in school. There is now a growing minority of boys who are growing up without a positive male role model, who are learning to expect that men no longer have the responsibilities of family or work, and who are more difficult to motivate and manage in school.

Social and economic changes may have generated a corresponding shift in the concerns of teaching staff and pupils. There is a growing consensus about the pre-eminent importance of basic literacy in mainstream special provision (Campbell and Neill, 1994). In the survey schools, both primary and secondary, there was not a single teacher who did not place reading difficulties as the highest priority for special provision. There was a feeling that, given the training and the resources, many would like to help poor attainers to read. Among the pupils, too, there was an increasing acceptance of the place of reading classes. As one recalled, 'At first I was embarrassed, but it was OK later. I couldn't have managed without it.'

This growing awareness of literacy problems has not meant that staff had forgotten the importance of access to the 'broad, balanced' curriculum – or the significance of exam accreditation in determining the life chances of marginalized pupils. This came across particularly strongly in the survey schools' discussions of the role of attendance in raising the pass rates of the least able in terms of GCSE and vocational qualifications. It was one of the main reasons why they wanted to include poor attenders among those identified in the SEN procedures and to devote more training and resources to their problems.

THE CONTEXT OF INTEGRATION

There was a recognition among some of the survey staff that for statemented pupils the problems of social polarization can be compounded. According to the previous Minister of State for the Disabled (Hague, 1994, personal communication), there were no official figures for employment rates among disabled school leavers, or for the income rates of those in work. Surveys do exist – for example, Kuh *et al.* (1988) and Hirst (1987) – and they indicate that the chances of employment for disabled school leavers are much lower than for the general population, even worse for those with additional learning difficulties and even worse still for those from special schools.

Special provision, particularly if it can be structured to involve a sizeable group of staff, can provide a channel for these concerns. One of the gravest weaknesses of the Code of Practice is that it abstracts the assessment of special needs from the experience of special provision. This book has argued that if, through a coordinated staffing and training strategy, mainstream teachers can learn how to integrate statemented pupils, they will become much more confident in their assessment of all pupils with special needs.

Well-inclined mainstream teachers can easily be trained in the teaching of reading and they are often as effective as 'experts' for all but a tiny minority of pupils. Many mainstream teachers have used Records of Achievement, personal and social education lessons or guidance and counselling to listen to and develop their understanding of statemented pupils. Given the time and the training, they enjoy the opportunity to develop differentiated materials and activities for them within their own areas of subject expertise, and they particularly relish the opportunity to teach them in a safe, supported small-group situation.

Another criticism levelled against the Code was that it has so little to say about integration. There were thirteen unsuccessful attempts between 1982 and 1994 to get anti-discrimination legislation for disabled people accepted in Parliament (Barnes and Oliver, 1995). When amendments were raised for William Hague's Bill in respect of integrated schooling, these were turned down on the grounds that the Code of Practice covered the issue. Many statemented pupils would prefer to be integrated, given the choice (Aspis, 1992). For some, like Isabel, removal from their local school can seem like 'the worst day of my life'.

SPECIAL PROVISION AS PROBLEM SOLVING

If special provision appeals to the heart, it can also present intellectual challenges. Present arrangements for LMS funding and parental choice mean that there are no easy answers for schools with large numbers of poorer families in areas of high deprivation (Vincent *et al.*, 1995). The Audit Commission's report on 'Access and achievement in urban schools' (DES, 1992) made clear that, despite exceptions, standards for children with special needs in these areas have failed to rise following the introduction of the National Curriculum.

If overall standards are to rise in the aftermath of the Code, much will depend on how rigorously Schedule Two of the Statutory

Instruments No. 1048 (DfE, 1994a) is enforced. This is designed to ensure that governing bodies provide information about the way that the resources which are devolved from LEAs in respect of pupils with SEN are actually spent. This may allow resources to be redistributed to the teaching of basic skills, to in-class support across the curriculum, to the development of more appropriate curricular differentiation and to staff workshops on special needs prevention, assessment and provision.

Schools which implemented the Warnock recommendations about staged assessment found that these rarely included sufficient curricular detail. The introduction of IEPs means that there will have to be regular reviews of teaching provision and learning needs for each of the pupils with special needs, even those with minor behavioural difficulties. This can be used as a springboard for problem solving across the curriculum (Butt and Scott, 1994).

The SENCo at Eastville, one of the survey schools which shared its special provision between a large number of mainstream teachers, divided the group into four teams and focused their attention on four main subjects for one term's support. Each of the staff involved agreed to produce up to six pieces of differentiated work for a specific pupil with special needs in the subject they were supporting. The LEA had provided a part time Advisory teacher for that term and she would be there for training and back-up. It was stressed that most of the pupils at Stages 1 and 2 of the assessment procedure had similar problems, and that in producing materials and activities for just one pupil they would probably help a much larger number. But by concentrating on the actual needs of one real pupil in their chosen subject, they would be able to look in much greater depth at the particular opportunities that the subject provided for pupils with special needs.

At the SEN workshop where this strategy was broached, two of the teachers immediately realized that this would enable the heads of those four departments to start a catalogue of differentiated materials. This catalogue could be used as the basis for the IEPs of those pupils – but also for work with many other pupils at Stage 1 of the assessment procedure who may not have an IEP. A third teacher countered that in emphasizing pupils' individual needs, IEPs could actually distract staff from the possibilities of integrative group activities, however. This teacher had spent her previous support lessons working with small groups of pupils, which included the more able as well as those with statements for moderate learning difficulties, on role play and drama, and these lessons had played a part in cementing the bonds between the pupils with special needs and those of the rest of the class – as well as communicating the lesson content more vividly.

At some schools, the SENCo is actively involved in the school's review of the behavioural policy (Bell and Best, 1988). At Eastville, the two key issues were seen as an agreement by all staff about what constituted the bottom line. Staff agreed that no pupil should refuse a request by a member of staff. Everything else flowed from that. The second issue was attendance. As a result, pupils with attendance problems were included in the staged assessment procedures, with positive results for attendance rates and SATs and GCSE scores.

At Southville, the SENCo was particularly concerned with a minority of more able and talented pupils. She had actively encouraged the special needs staff to contribute their ideas about recruiting more of such pupils to a school which had a good reputation for special provision. The answer they came up with was to promote differentiation and in-class support as a means of extending the work of the more able and talented. At that school, the more able were monitored at Stages 1 and 2 of the SEN assessment process and their progress was reviewed as regularly as pupils with learning difficulties. Close contact was maintained between the school and their parents, just as it was between the school and the parents of the less able and those with behavioural difficulties. There were individual interviews, but also meetings, with invited speakers, to introduce courses on thinking skills and to help parents understand the demands of SATs and GCSEs and to enable them to support their children in their revision programmes. Information about these developments was then added to the school's prospectus, to enable it to respond to a competitor school in a more affluent part of the town which promoted Latin as a way of recruiting the more able.

A SECOND DRAFT CODE?

For all its strengths, and despite the sense of renewed confidence that greeted its publication, many SENCos feel that the Code of Practice neglected the issues of SEN resourcing and definition, teacher retraining and the polarization of pupil recruitment. In focusing on the procedures of identification and assessment, it lacked a wider vision of special educational provision. It offered a potentially daunting increase in paperwork for SENCos, who try to shoulder the whole burden on their own. And in its ambiguities about the thresholds between the various stages, it sidestepped the problems of equity and consistency in special provision.

Some of the schools featured in the survey treated the Code as if it were the second in a series of drafts. They were willing to harness their colleagues' 'expressions of concern' to develop a coordinated staffing and training strategy. They were sharing SEN assessment between these staff and reducing the paperwork. They were looking at common screening tests and checklists of those aspects of special needs, like behavioural and emotional difficulties, that were not amenable to quick and easy group tests, in order to create an LEA moderated register. And they shared a concern for the wider social and political issues of polarization and marginalization of low attaining pupils in areas of increasing social deprivation.

There was considerable anxiety about the pressures brought to bear on schools to become rather more 'exclusive'. There was a concern about the effects this was having on pupils with special needs and, through them, on society as a whole. The survey schools felt that competition generated by league tables of exam results and the present regulations for parental choice hindered their work on SEN prevention and provision. It meant they had to make themselves more attractive to the more affluent and upwardly mobile parents. Schools with a good reputation for special provision were losing their more able pupils. One approach which was gaining favour was redefining special provision to include the more able and talented pupils and calling all the pupils involved 'exceptional children' (Dunn, 1972; Hallahan and Kauffmann, 1991). But there was also a feeling that if other government reforms in education were to be reconciled with high quality special provision for statemented and non-statemented pupils in the majority of mainstream schools, there would need to be a wholesale new reconstruction of the Code.

Bibliography

Arnold, H. (1982) *Listening to Children Reading*. London: Hodder & Stoughton.

Ashcroft, P. (1986) Personal communication.

Aspis, S. (1992) Integration. *Disability, Handicap and Society* **7** (3), 281–3.

Assessment of Performance Unit (APU) (1987) *The Assessment of Reading*. Windsor: NFER-Nelson.

Ball, S. *et al.* (1994) Competitive schooling: values, ethics and cultural engineering. *Journal of Curriculum and Supervision* **9** (4), 350–67.

Barnes, C. and Oliver, M. (1995) Disability rights: rhetoric and reality in the UK. *Disability and Society* **10** (1), 111–16.

Barrett, J. (1994) Reading with Mother. *Reading* **20**, 173–8.

Barton, L. (1986) The politics of special needs. *Disability, Handicap and Society* **1** (3), 273–90.

Beard, R. *Teaching Literacy: Balancing Perspectives*. London: Hodder & Stoughton.

Becker, H. (1963) *The Other Side*. London: Macmillan.

Becker, W. (1977) Teaching reading and language to the disadvantaged. *Harvard Educational Review* **47** (4).

Bell, P. and Best, R. (1988) *Supportive Education*. Oxford: Blackwell.

Bibby, P. (1994) Dreamland of special needs draft. *Times Educational Supplement*, 18 February, 8.

Bines, H. (1986) *Redefining Remedial Education*. Beckenham: Croom Helm.

Blagg, N. *et al.* (1988) *Somerset Thinking Skills Course*. Oxford: Blackwell.

Booth, T., Potts, P. and Swann, W. (1987) *Preventing Difficulties in Learning*. Oxford: Blackwell.

Bradshaw, J. (1990) *Child Poverty and Deprivation in the UK*. UNICEF.

Brooks, G. *et al.* (1992) In Gorman, T. (ed.) *What Teachers in Training Are Taught About Reading*. Windsor: NFER-Nelson.

Brophy, J. and Good, T. (1974) *Teacher Student Relationship: Causes and Consequences*. Holt.

Brown, D. (1994) Truants, families and schools. *Educational Review* **35** (3).

Brown, S. (1994) Multiple policy innovations: the impact on special educational needs provision. *British Journal of Special Education* **21** (3), 97–100.

Bryant, P. (1990) Rhyme, language and children's reading. *Applied Psycholinguistics* **11**, 237–52.

Butt, N. and Scott, E.M. (1994) Individual education plans in secondary schools. *Support for Learning* **9** (1), 70–2.

Campbell, J. and Neill, S. (1994) *Curriculum Reform at Key Stage 1: Teacher Commitment and Policy Failure*. Harlow: Longman.

Canter, L. (1992) *Assertive Discipline*. USA: Lee Canter and Associates.

Chapman, E.K. and Stone, J.M. (1988) *The Visually Handicapped Child in Your Classroom*. London: Cassell.

Chorley, D. (1993) OFSTED prepares for special inspections. *British Journal of Special Education* **20** (4), 127–8.

Clay, M. (1979) *Reading: The Patterning of Complex Behaviour*. London: Heinemann.

Clay, M. (1990) The Reading Recovery Programme: 1984–8. *New Zealand Journal of Educational Studies* **25**, 61–70.

Collins, J.E. (1961) *The Effects of Remedial Education*. Edinburgh: Oliver & Boyd.

Cooper, C. (1993) *The Workplace Revolution*. London: Kogan Page.

Cooper, P. (1993) Learning from pupils' perspectives. *British Journal of Special Education* **20** (4), 129–33.

Csapo, M. and Goguen, L. (1980) *Special Education Across Canada*. Vancouver: Centre for Human Development and Research.

Dalton, J. (1994) Special magic needed to crack code. *Times Educational Supplement*, 20 May, 20.

Dearing, R. (1993) *The National Curriculum and Its Assessment*. London: SCAA.

Department for Education (DfE) (1993a) *Access and Achievement in Urban Schools*. London: HMSO.

DfE (1993b) *Education Act 1993*. London: HMSO.

DfE (1994a) *Code of Practice on the Identification and Assessment of Special Educational Needs*. London: Central Office of Information.

DfE (1994b) *The Organisation of Special Educational Provision*. Circular 6/94. London: Central Office of Information.

Department of Education and Science (DES) (1975) *A Language for Life* (Bullock Report). London: HMSO.

DES (1978) *Special Educational Needs* (Warnock Report). London: HMSO.

DES (1988) *Education Reform Act*. London: HMSO.

DES (1989a) *Discipline in Schools* (Elton Report). London: HMSO.

DES (1989b) *Records of Achievement*. RANSC.

DES (1990) *Staffing for Pupils with Special Educational Needs*. Circular 11/90. London: HMSO.

DES (1992) *Getting in on the Act*. London: Audit Commission/HMI/HMSO.

Desforges, M. and Lindsay, G. (1995) *Infants Index*. London: Hodder & Stoughton.

Dexter, L. (1963) 'On the politics and sociology of stupidity in our society'. In Becker (1963).

Dolan, T. *et al.* (1979) 'Improving reading through group discussion activities'. In Lunzer, E. and Gardner, K. (eds) *The Effective Use of Reading*. London: Heinemann.

Dunn, L. (1972) *Exceptional Children in the Schools*. New York: Holt, Rinehart and Winston.

Dyson, A. (1993) Innovatory mainstream practice: what's happening in schools' provision for special needs? *Support for Learning* 7 (2), 51–7.

Dyson, A. and Gains, C. (1995) The role of the special needs coordinator: poisoned chalice or crock of gold? *Support for Learning* 10 (2), 50–6.

Evans, J. and Lunt, J. (1994) Special educational provision after LMS. *British Journal of Special Education* 21 (3), 97–100.

Feuerstein, R. (1980) *Instrumental Enrichment*. Baltimore: University Park Press.

Fordham, D. (1989) Flexibility in the National Curriculum. *British Journal of Special Education* 16 (2), 50–2.

Foster, G., Ysseldyke, J. and Reese, J. (1972) 'I wouldn't have seen it, if I hadn't believed it'. *Exceptional Children* 63, 617–24.

Fox, G. (1993) *A Handbook for Special Needs Assistants*. London: David Fulton.

Francis, D. and Turkington, R. (1992) Balancing the Act. *Special Children* 53, 23–6.

Fraser, C. (1984) 'The follow up study: psychological aspects'. In Illsley, R. and Mitchell, R.G. (eds) *Low Birth Weight: A Medical, Psychological and Social Study*. Wiley.

Fry, E. (1977) Fry's readability graph. *Journal of Reading* 21, 242–52.

Garner, P. (1994) Exclusions from schools. *Pastoral Care* 12, 3–10.

Garner, P. (1995) Sense or nonsense? Dilemmas in the SEN Code of Practice. *Support for Learning* 10 (1), 3–7.

Gold, D. (1994) 'We don't call it a circle': the ethos of a support group. *Disability and Society* 9 (4), 435–52.

Goodman, K. (1993) *Language and Literacy*. London: Routledge & Kegan Paul.

Gross, J. (1993) *Special Educational Needs in the Primary School: A Practical Guide*. Milton Keynes: Open University Press.

Gulliford, R. and Upton, G. (eds) (1992) *Special Educational Needs*. London: Routledge.

Hallahan, D.P. and Kauffmann, J.M. (1991) *Exceptional Children: Introduction to Special Education*. Boston: Allyn & Bacon.

Handy, C. (1993) *The Age of Unreason*. London: Century Business.

Hanko, G. (1993) *Special Needs in Ordinary Classrooms*. Oxford: Blackwell.

Hannam, C. *et al.* (1984) *Young Teachers and Reluctant Learners*. Harmondsworth: Penguin.

Harvey, J. (1995) The role of the special needs coordinator at Marton Grove Primary School. *Support for Learning* 10 (2), 79–82.

Hegarty, S. *Meeting Special Needs in Ordinary Schools*. London: Cassell.

Her Majesty's Inspectorate (HMI) (1992) *Special Needs Issues*. London: HMSO.

Hirst, M. (1987) Careers of young people with disabilities: between the ages of 15 and 21. *Disability, Handicap and Society* 2 (1), 61–74.

Holt, J. (1964) *How Children Fail*. Harmondsworth: Penguin.

Hornby, G., Davis, G. and Taylor, G. (1995) *The Special Educational Needs Coordinator's Handbook*. London: Routledge.

Hornsby, B. and Shear, F. (1975) *Alpha to Omega: The A-Z of Teaching Reading*. London: Heinemann.

Hugill, B. (1995) State GCSE pupils fall behind. *Observer*, 30 July.

Jordan, E. (1994) The special educational needs of traveller children. *Bridges* **2** (1), 17–18.

Kuh, D., Lawrence, C., Tripp, J. and Creber, G. (1988) Work and work alternatives for disabled young people. *Disability, Handicap and Society* **3** (1), 3–26.

Lake, M. (1991) Surveying all the factors. *Language and Learning*, 8–23.

Landy, M. (1994) Preparation for school inspection. *Support for Learning* **9** (1), 3–8.

Lawrence, B. (1991) Self concept formation and physical handicap: some educational implications for integration. *Disability, Handicap and Society* **6** (2), 139–46.

Lawrence, D. (1973) *Improved Reading Through Counselling*. London: Ward-Lock.

Lingard, T. (1994) The acquisition of literacy in secondary education. *British Journal of Special Education* **4**, 180–91.

Lipman, M. (1980) *Philosophy in the Classroom*. Philadelphia: Temple University Press.

Lunt, I., Evans, J., Norwich, B. and Weddell, K. (1994) *Working Together: Inter School Collaboration for Special Needs*. London: David Fulton.

McAvoy, D. (1994) Interview, Radio Cleveland. July.

Male, J. and Thompson, C. (1985) *The Educational Implications of Disability*. RADAR.

Mintzberg, H. (1973) *The Nature of Managerial Work*. London: Harper & Row.

Mittler, P. (1992) Educational entitlement in the nineties. *Support for Learning* **7** (4), 141–51.

Mittler, P. (1994) A post-code address. *Times Educational Supplement*, 13 May.

MORI (1994) Survey for Radio 1FM, *The Big Holy One: Do the Right Thing*. October.

Moss, G. (ed.) (1995) *The Basics of Special Needs*. London: Routledge.

National Curriculum Council (NCC) (1989) *A Curriculum for All*. London: NCC.

Newbolt Report (1921) London: HMSO.

Nolan, C. (1987) *Under the Eye of the Clock*. London: Weidenfeld and Nicolson.

OFSTED (1993) *Access and Achievement in Urban Schools*. London: HMSO.

OFSTED (1995) *Chief Inspector's Annual Report*. London: HMSO.

O'Grady (1993) Seeing is believing. *Times Educational Supplement*.

O'Keefe, D.J. (1994) *Truancy in English Secondary Schools*. London: HMSO.

Oliver, M. (1992) Changing the social relations of research production. *Disability, Handicap and Society* **7** (2), 107–14.

Peter, M. (ed.) (1992) Differentiation: ways forward. *British Journal of Special Education* **19** (1).

Peters, T. and Waterman, R. (1982) *In Search of Excellence*. London: Harper & Row.

Pickup, M. (1995) The role of the special needs coordinator: developing philosophy and practice. *Support for Learning* **10** (2), 88–92.

Plackett, E. (1991) *The English Curriculum: Reading 2: Slow Readers.* The English Centre.

Power, C. Manor, O. and Fox, J. (1991) *Health and Class.* London: Chapman and Hall.

Powney, J. and Watts, M. (1987) *Interviewing in Educational Research.* London: Routledge & Kegan Paul.

Pumfrey, P. and Mittler, P. (1989) Peeling off the labels. *Times Educational Supplement,* 13 October.

Pumfrey, P. and Reason, R. (1991) *Specific Learning Difficulties (Dyslexia): Challenges and Responses.* Windsor: NFER-Nelson.

Rabinowicz, J. and Friel, J. (1994) The new tribunal: the first responses. *British Journal of Special Education* **21** (1), 27–8.

Robertson, A., King, L. and Sewell, G. (1995) *SEN Moderation Project.* Cleveland LEA.

Russell, P. (1994) The Code of Practice: new partnerships for children with special educational needs. *British Journal of Special Education* **21** (2), 48–52.

Rutter, M. and Smith, D. (1995) *Psychosocial Disorders in Young People.* Chichester: John Wiley.

Salvia, J. and Ysseldyke, J.E. (1985) *Assessment in Special and Remedial Education.* Boston: Houghton Mifflin.

Sayer, J. (1994) *Secondary Schools for All? Strategies for Special Needs.* 2nd edn. London: Cassell.

Schutz, A. (1964) 'The stranger: an essay in social psychology'. In Broderson, A. (ed.) *Studies in Social Theory.* Leiden: Nijhoff.

Secondary Heads Association (SHA) (1990) *Managing Special Needs.* Bristol: SHA.

Sewell, G. (1982) *Reshaping Remedial Education.* Beckenham: Croom Helm.

Sewell, G. (1988) 'Free flow and the secondary school'. In Thomas and Feiler.

Simmons, K. (1986) Painful extractions. *Times Educational Supplement.*

Simmons, K. (1994) Decoding a new message. *British Journal of Special Education* **21** (2), 56–9.

Skrtic, T. (1991) *Behind Special Education: A Critical Analysis of Professional Culture and School Organization.* Denver: Love.

Smith, C.J. and Laslett, R. (1993) *Effective Classroom Management: A Teacher's Guide.* London: Routledge.

Smith, F. (1986) *Reading.* Cambridge: Cambridge University Press.

Sutton, R. *et al.* (1986) *Assessment in Secondary Schools: The Manchester Experience.* London: Longman.

Swann, W. (1985) Is the integration of children with special needs happening? *Oxford Review of Education* **11** (1), 3–18.

Swann, W. (1988) 'Learning difficulties and curriculum reform: integration or differentiation?' In Thomas and Feiler.

TES (1995) Complaints pour in over national test results. *Times Educational Supplement,* July.

Thomas, D. (1978) *The Social Psychology of Childhood Disability*. London: Methuen.

Thomas, G. and Feiler, A. (1988) *Planning for Special Needs*. Oxford: Blackwell.

Thomas, R.M. (1985) 'Body image and body language'. In *The International Encyclopaedia of Education*. Oxford: Oxford University Press.

Toffler, A. (1980) *The Third Wave*. New York: William Morrow.

Tomlinson, S. (1982) *A Sociology of Special Education*. London: Routledge & Kegan Paul.

Topping, K.J. (1986) *Parents as Educators: Training Parents to Teach Their Children*. Beckenham: Croom Helm.

Townsend, P. (1991) 'The poor are poorer: a statistical report on changes in the living standards of rich and poor in the United Kingdom: 1979–1989'. University of Bristol.

Vincent, C., Evans, J., Lunt, I. and Young, P. (1995) Policy and practice: the changing nature of special educational provision in schools. *British Journal of Special Education* 22 (1).

Visser, J. (1986) Support: A description of the work of the SEN professional. *Support for Learning* 1, 6–9.

Walters, B. (1994) *Management for Special Needs*. London: Cassell.

Warnock, M. (1994) Crack the Code for the vulnerable 20%. *Times Educational Supplement*.

Webster, A. and Wood, D. (1989) *Children with Hearing Difficulties*. London: Cassell.

Wedell, K. (1993) The Draft Code of Practice. *British Journal of Special Education* 20 (4), 119.

Westwood, P. (1993) *Commonsense Methods for Children with Special Needs*. London: Routledge.

Wilcox, B. and Eustace, P.J. (1980) *Tooling up for Curriculum Review*. Windsor: NFER.

Wilkinson, A. (1988) *An Introduction to the National Oracy Project*. York: NCC.

Wilkinson, R.G. (1994) *Unfair Shares*. London: Barnardo's.

Wolfendale, S. (1992) *Empowering Parents and Teachers*. London: Cassell.

Appendix 1

```
┌─────────────┐
│  EASTVILLE  │
│   SCHOOL    │
└─────────────┘
```

SPECIAL NEEDS

HIGHLY CONFIDENTIAL STAGE 1 REGISTER

R: READING B: = BEHAVIOUR   H: = HEARING   ME: MEDICAL   P: P.H.

W: WRITING A: = ATTENDANCE   S: = SIGHT

M: MATHS   G: = GIFTED

	R	W	M	B	A	G	H	S	ME	P

EASTVILLE SCHOOL
INDIVIDUAL EDUCATION PLAN

Name of child ....   Date of birth ....

Class ....   ☐ Stage 2   ☐ Stage 3

Summary of needs :-

Targets :-

Action plan :-

a) Help/Support

b) Staff to be involved

c) Curricular arrangements

Medical :-

Agency support :-

Parents signature ....   This individual educational plan will be
                                                                 reviewed :- ....
Pupils signature ....

Staff signature ....   Date ....

EASTVILLE SCHOOL
INDIVIDUAL EDUCATION PLAN

Name of child ....   Date of birth ....

Class ....   ☐ Stage 2   ☐ Stage 3

Summary of needs :-

Targets :-

Action plan :-

a) Help/Support

b) Staff to be involved

c) Curricular arrangements

Medical :-

Agency support :-

Parents views :-

Pupils views :-

Parents signature ....
Pupils signature ....
Staff signature ....

This individual educational plan will be
reviewed :- ....
Date ....

2

EASTVILLE SCHOOL

INDIVIDUAL EDUCATION PLAN

PARENTS COMMENTS

Name of child ....   Date of birth ....

Class ....   ☐ Stage 2   ☐ Stage 3

Parents views :-

Summary of needs :-

Targets :-

Childs views :-

Summary of needs :-

Targets :-

Parents signature ....

Pupils signature ....

Staff signature ....

This individual educational plan will be reviewed :- ....

Date ....

EASTVILLE SCHOOL

READING PROFILE   **HIGHLY CONFIDENTIAL**

NAME : ....   CLASS : ....

R A   Sept .... (Gapadol)   R A   Dec .... (GAP)

Books Read : 1 ....

         2 ....

         3 ....

Accuracy : (% and Date) ....
....

Errors : ....
....

Types of Errors : eg too fast, first letter and guess, omission, reversal, insert, grammar,
mispronouncing : ....
....
....

Long and Unfamiliar Words : ....
....

Self Corrections :

Confidence :

Fluency :

Literal Comprehension :

Inference :

Use of Context Cues :

Letter Sounds not known :

Reading Profile Summary :
....
....
....
....

SIGNED :   **DATE :**

EASTVILLE SCHOOL
INDIVIDUAL EDUCATION PLAN REVIEW

Name of child ....   Date of birth ....

Class ....   Date of review ....

Progress review :-

Future targets :-

Parents views :-

Pupils views :-

Review decision :-

☐   Remain at stage 2/3

☐   Move to stage 3

☐   Revert to stage 1/2

☐   Request formal assessment

Parents signature ....

Pupils signature ....

Staff signature ....

Appendix 2
SEN Code framework descriptors and prescriptions

	Prevention and Preparation	Stage 1 trigger	Resources under action plan	Evidence gathering	Stage 2 trigger	Resources under IEP	External agencies	Stage 3 trigger	Resources under IEP	External agencies	Stage 4 trigger	External agencies
Cognitive functioning and IQ	Medical data Pre-school data Screening data	Class teacher, health, SSD or parental concern	Special attention and differentiation in class, home liaison	Class records, NC attainments, standardized tests, profile and teacher observation	Working significantly below level of peers: Level 1 at 8, Level 2 at 11	Up to 10% small-group or in-class support for one term	CPS advice, LSS advice	No progress despite additional help	Up to 20% small-group or in-class support for one term	CPS assessment	Referral by school, parent or agency	CPS, LEA, medical, SSD and other agencies
Communication skills	Speech therapy records	Class teacher, health, SSD or parental concern especially speech therapist	Special attention in class, liaison with parents	NC attainments profile, medical data, parent perceptions	Evidence of communication difficulties affecting learning or relationships	Speech therapy advice	Speech therapy advice	No progress despite advice	Speech therapy advice	CPS assessment	Referral by school, parent or agency	CPS, LEA, medical, SSD and other agencies
Reading	Reading policy Reading records	Class teacher, health, SSD or parental concern	Differentiated texts and activities in class, home liaison	Reading scores, NC attainments, teacher observation	Working two years below level of peers: RA 6 at 8, RA 9.5 at 11.5	Up to 10% small-group or in-class support for one term	LSS advice and action	No progress on extreme problems RA 5 at 8, RA 7.5 at 11.5	Up to 20% help for a wider repertoire of approaches on LSS advice	CPS assessment	Referral by school, parent or agency	CPS, LEA, medical, SSD and other agencies
Writing, spelling and handwriting	Writing policy Spelling policy Writing records	Class teacher or parental concern	Differentiated tasks and strategies in class, home liaison	Copies of pupil's writing, spelling scores, NC attainments	Working two years below level of peers: SA 6 at 8, SA 9 at 11.5	One lesson a week of in-class help for one term, IT support	LSS advice and action	No progress despite additional help and advice	A wider range of approaches based on LSS advice	CPS assessment	Referral by school, parent or agency	CPS, LEA, medical, SSD and other agencies

SEN Code framework descriptors and prescriptions — *contd.*

	Prevention and Preparation	Stage 1 trigger	Resources under action plan	Evidence gathering	Stage 2 trigger	Resources under IEP	External agencies	Stage 3 trigger	Resources under IEP	External agencies	Stage 4 trigger	External agencies
Educational attainments	Marking policy Assessment policy/SATs records	Class teacher or parental concern	Differentiated tasks and special attention in class, home liaison	Copies of pupil's work, NC attainments, teacher observation	Working below level of peers: Level 1 at 8 Level 2 at 11	Up to 10% small-group or in-class support for one term: IT	CPS advice	No progress despite additional help and advice	A wider range of approaches: up to 20% help	CPS assessment	Referral by school, parent or agency	CPS, LEA, medical, SSD and other agencies
Specific learning difficulties	IQ scores Speech records Reading and spelling records	Class teacher or parental concern	Differentiated tasks and special attention in class, home liaison	Teacher observation, parental views, test scores, NC attainments	Significant discrepancy between oral ability and reading/spelling/maths	Up to 10% small-group or in-class support for one term: IT	LSS advice and action	Discrepancy of two standard deviations between IQ and RA/SA	A wider range of approaches based on LSS support	CPS assessment	Referral by school, parent or agency	CPS, LEA, medical, SSD and other agencies
More able and talented	MAT policy Equal opportunities IQ scores	Class teacher or parental concern	Differentiated tasks and special attention in class, home liaison	Teacher observation, parental views, test scores, NC attainments			CPS advice					
Behaviour	PSE programme Behaviour policy Guidance and counselling programme	Class teacher, health, SSD or parental concern	Discussion of problems with child and parents: targets met	Teacher observation, parental views, pupil views, evidence of incidents	Bullying, anti-social behaviour, refusal to work despite parental support	Weekly counselling by teacher, pastoral staff or agencies	CPS advice, BSS advice and action	Frequent involvement of parents: exclusions regular anti-social incidents well recorded	A wider range of approaches based on CPS and BSS advice	CPS assessment	Referral by school, parent or agency	CPS, LEA, medical, SSD and other agencies

	Prevention and Preparation	Stage 1 trigger	Resources under action plan	Evidence gathering	Stage 2 trigger	Resources under IEP	External agencies	Stage 3 trigger	Resources under IEP	External agencies	Stage 4 trigger	External agencies
Emotional state	PSE programme Guidance and counselling programme	Class teacher, health, SSD or parental concern	Discussion of problems with child and parents: targets met	Teacher observation, parental views, pupil views, evidence of incidents	Withdrawn, anxious, low self-esteem despite parental support	Weekly counselling by teacher, pastoral staff or agencies	CPS advice, GP advice, BSS advice and action	No progress despite additional help and advice	A wider range of approaches based on CPS and LSS	CPS assessment	Referral by school, parent or agency	CPS, LEA, medical, SSD and other advice
Attendance	Attendance policy	Class teacher, health, SSD or ESW and parental concern	Discussion of problems with child and parents targets met	Attendance records			ESW					
Physical health	Medical data Pre-school data	Class teacher, health, SSD and parental concern	Special attention in school, discussion of problems	Teacher observation, parental and pupil views, medical records	Health problems affecting attendance and progress	Physical aids and access, IT	School nurse advice, medical advice	Concern from external agencies	Short-term adaptations and NC	GP and SCMO	Referral by school, parent or agency	CPS, LEA, medical, SSD and other advice
Mobility	Medical data Pre-school data	Class teacher, health, SSD and parental concern	Special attention in school: discussion of problems	School audit, teacher observation, parental views, pupil views, medical records	Inability to access school or curriculum without help	Physical aids and IT and access	Medical advice	Concern from external agencies	Short-term adaptations and NC	SCMO assessment and GP	Referral by school, parent or agency	CPS, LEA, medical, SSD and other advice

SEN Code framework descriptors and prescriptions — *contd.*

	Prevention and Preparation	Stage 1 trigger	Resources under action plan	Evidence gathering	Stage 2 trigger	Resources under IEP	External agencies	Stage 3 trigger	Resources under IEP	External agencies	Stage 4 trigger	External agencies
Developmental function	Medical data Pre-school data	Class teacher, health, SSD and parental concern	Special attention in school: discussion of problems	School audit, teacher observation, parental views, pupil views, medical records	Inability to access school or curriculum without help	Access to WC	Medical advice	Concern from external agencies	Short-term adaptations and NC	SCMO assessment and GP	Referral by school, parent or agency	CPS, LEA, medical, SSD and other advice
Hearing	Medical data Previous records	Class teacher, HI teacher, health, SSD and parental concern	Special attention in class discussion of problems	Medical records, HI reports, teacher, parent and pupil views	Hearing loss up to 50 db	Hearing aids as appropriate	HI advice and action	Concern from external agencies	Short-term adaptations and NC	HI, CPS	Referral by school, parent or agency	CPS, LEA, medical, SSD and other advice
Vision	Medical data Previous records	Class teacher, VI teacher, health, SSD and parental concern	Special attention in class: discussion of problems	Medical reports, VI reports, teacher, parent and pupil views	Visual problems up 20/200	Lighting	VI advice and action	Concern from external agencies	Short-term adaptations and NC	VI, CPS	Referral by school, parent or agency	CPS, LEA, medical, SSD and other advice

Name Index

Subject Index